THE

WORLD'S GREATEST

NAME

THE
WORLD'S GREATEST
NAME

The Names and Titles of
Jesus Christ
H. I. J. K.

by Charles J. Rolls

LOIZEAUX BROTHERS
Neptune, New Jersey

REVISED EDITION, OCTOBER 1984
THIRD PRINTING, MAY 1989

Earlier edition, ©Zondervan 1956

Library of Congress Cataloging in Publication Data

Rolls, Charles J. (Charles Jubilee), 1887-
    The world's greatest name: The names and titles of
Jesus Christ: H—K. Revised edition.

    1. Jesus Christ—Name. I. Title. II. Series:
Rolls, Charles J. (Charles Jubilee), 1887-   Names
and titles of Jesus Christ.

BT590.N2R622 1984   232   84-15416
ISBN 0-87213-732-5

PRINTED IN THE UNITED STATES OF AMERICA

To
Miss Marie Loizeaux

to whom I am deeply indebted
for having devoted the painstaking labor
of her skillful ability
in the reediting of the first three volumes of my work
on the names, titles, and vocations of Christ

this book is dedicated

CONTENTS

H

I

7

J

K

FOREWORD

No mind in any race or realm of mankind possesses the capacity to describe, or the capability to declare the glories of the Christ of God. No other character reflects so many facets of truth, no other commander controls so many spheres of administration, and no other celebrity maintains such widespread dominion as competently as Christ does. The splendid bearing of His blameless life, the spacious blessings of His faultless ministry, and the changeless function of His ceaseless mediation place Him forever beyond the range of equality with any leader or legislator. Christ has a personality that cannot be qualified or compared. If we examine His service on earth His deeds were always wrought at the most opportune moment, in the most appropriate manner, without exception. Never once during His entire labors is there a single instance of His being in a hurry, of acting impatiently, or of arriving too late to achieve His purpose. Throughout His ministry He did not need to minimize the meaning of any statement He made, amend His message, repeal an utterance, or revise a sentence. His teaching was independent of the age in which He lived, and did not rely for its accuracy on any advisory counsel. He ministered forgiveness to many, but never asked pardon of any. So fitly and finally did Christ fulfill the law and the prophets, that no one more competent and comely, and bearing so many marks of reality, could possibly be manifested to mankind.

Loftier and lovelier than all leaders, more durable and desirable than all dignitaries, the Son of Man bears a Name that is above every name. Every torch that renders testimony to God's greatness and goodness has been lit by His light, every tie of amiable affection existing among men has been knit by His kind and kingly love, while all trends that lend triumph to

11

high endeavor have been tutored by the victorious virtue of His perfect life. The fame of His excellent name is reflected through the flaming stars of the heavens, the flying birds of the air, the flowing streams of the hills, the fruitful trees of the field, and the fragrant flowers of springtime. He writes His message of salvation in letters large and legible, so as to direct our footsteps to Himself the Saviour, the sole fount of true freedom and felicity. The Son of Man justly merits the highest praise and worthiest worship we can possibly render, and we should gladly combine with these the deepest gratitude and holiest reverence, when attempting to magnify His glorious name.

> The fountain of His fullness never fails
> The reservoir of His resource never recedes
> The wisdom of His Word never wanes
> The vigor of His virtue never varies
> The burnish of His beauty never blemishes
> The luster of His love never lessens
> The prowess of His power never perishes

In view of many letters to hand from Christian workers the world over, expressing appreciation for devotional help received through reading *The Indescribable Christ,* this further volume on the names and titles of our blessed Lord is sent forth, with the hope that it will prove an instrument of the Spirit in promoting greater heart affection for Him who is at the right hand of God.

                                        C. J. ROLLS

H

These names portray Christ in superior Headship as highest and holiest in both honor and humility. He dignifies every high office and noble rank with marked distinction.

THE HIGHEST HIMSELF (Ps. 87:5)
> Excellence is exceeded and majesty magnified.

THE HOLY ONE AND JUST (Acts 3:14)
> A character unblemished, a conduct untarnished.

THE HOPE OF ISRAEL (Jer. 17:3)
> The Victor who assures triumph o'er the tomb.

THE HEAD OF THE CHURCH (Col. 1:18)
> Christ perfectly fills every office with dignity and durability.

THE HEIFER WITHOUT BLEMISH (Num. 19:3)
> A Sacrifice unrivaled in purity and unparalleled in history.

THE HEALER OF MEN (Ex. 15:26)
> Tender and trustworthy in time of trial.

THE HIGHWAY OF LIFE (Is. 35:8)
> Christ has established a way of access to the Father.

THE HEIR OF ALL THINGS (Heb. 1:2)
> The sole Possessor and supreme Proprietor.

THE HELPER OF THE NEEDY (Heb. 13:6)
> Strength and sympathy assured forever.

THE HE GOAT (Prov. 30:31)
> The Sanctifier who sustains spiritual society.

THE HIGH PRIEST FOREVER (Heb. 6:20)
> The Maintainer of mediatorial ministry.

THE HERALD OF THE GLAD TIDINGS (Is. 52:7)
> The perfect Witness to the will and work of God.

HE IS THE HEAD OF THE BODY, THE CHURCH

His Headship by appointment	*(Mark 12:10-11)*
His Headship by agreement	*(Col. 2:9)*
His Headship by arrangement	*(Eph. 5:23)*
His Headship by assignment	*(Eph. 1:21-23)*
His Headship by attainment	*(Col. 2:10)*
His Headship by atonement	*(Col. 1:18-20)*
His Headship by announcement	*(1 Cor. 11:3)*

THE HEAD OF EVERY MAN IS CHRIST

Head of the stars and sea, Head of the powers that be,
Head of Mankind is He, Head of eternity.

Head of the Church His Bride, Head of all things beside,
Head of the winds and tide, Head of the glorified.

Head of the plan of grace, Head of the human race,
Head with His sun-like face, Head of our resting place.

Head of Emmanuel's Land, Head of the Heavenly strand,
Head at our God's right hand, Head of the martyr band.

Head of the King's highway, Head of yon fadeless day,
Head where the righteous say, Thou art our strength
   and stay.

Head of the lords of earth, Head of the second birth,
Head by His peerless worth, Head of eternal mirth.

Head when the morning dawns, Head tho' once crowned
   with thorns,
Head when all death shall cease, Head of the reign of peace.

Head of all joy and bliss, Head of God's righteousness,
Head of holiness too, and Head of all things new.

C. J. R.

I am Alpha and Omega (Rev. 22:13)

Christ surpasses all other worthies that have gone before, both in His primal moral glory and personal mediative grace. In His inherent capacity and capability He holds precedence and preeminence above all the dignified of the centuries, for He is King of the ages (1 Tim. 1:17). He incorporates in His matchless character the combined qualities of sympathy, sufficiency, and superiority to a degree of perfection difficult for our minds to comprehend. His personal characteristics were not cramped by local and parochial boundaries, His capacities were not curtailed by racial or national confines, His teaching was not curbed by the temporal and transient conceptions of mankind, and His vision and virtue were not cultivated in the secular or sectarian colleges of this world. As Chief Shepherd, Christ excels in love and care all other custodians and caretakers, and He exceeds in wisdom and knowledge all other guardians and guides.

In eminence and efficiency He stands without equal in excellence, filling every office effectively; while in power and purpose He is without peer in perfection, discharging every obligation faithfully. In the exercise of His abiding authority He is forever free from all apology, apathy, and animosity in any form. His forceful leadership is fragrant in faithfulness and fervent in friendship. By virtue of His self-abnegating sacrifice He has secured salvation, established peace, promoted faith, imparted power, awakened hope, dispensed grace, constrained service, assured guidance, begotten courage, and pledged victory over all opposition and oppression.

With a distinguished deportment Christ displayed His divine dignity throughout the discharge of His earthly ministry. He never once asked for prayer or pity for Himself. He had no need to acknowledge a fault, confess a failure, or ask forgiveness from anyone, anywhere, at any time. His blameless character, stainless life, and faultless labor were all with one accord beyond reproach. No inequality marred the blended and balanced virtues of His noble character, no inability mutilated the strong and stately vigor of His courteous conduct, and no instability menaced the calm and confident voice of His stately command. Nothing about His capabilities was disproportionate, defective, or dwarfed, every capacity was complete, every ability entire, and every faculty perfect. No attribute of His personal competence, in action or expression, detracted from any other of His spiritual qualifications or credentials.

Our Lord is eminently fitted, expressly suited, and eternally qualified to be the Saviour of the sinful, the Shepherd of the sheep, and the Sovereign of the sanctified society, in the everlasting kingdom. His kingdom is a kingdom of spiritual truth, sovereign power, sublime love, steadfast righteousness, and supernal joy and is therefore destined to abide forever.

We now come to a group of our Lord's titles and offices beginning with the letter H.

THE HIGHEST HIMSELF

> Of Zion it shall be said, This and that man was born in her: and the Highest Himself shall establish her (Ps. 87:5).

The birth of the gracious Messiah and the beneficence of His glorious majesty are both introduced in this Psalm. Primarily, the privileges of citizenship and rights of heirship are the outcome of natural birthright, but in this case they are secured on the ground of supernatural law, even by regeneration. Luke is careful to designate the One manifested at Bethlehem "the Highest," which title he makes use of on seven occasions.

Messiah Himself is the founder of the City of God and the furnisher of all its privileges. The Son is rightfully "heir of all things" (Heb. 1:2); and although we were by nature without right and devoid of merit or claim as being aliens, we have, nevertheless, been called into the fellowship of His Son Jesus Christ our Lord, and are now fellow citizens with the saints and of the household of God (1 Cor. 1:9; Eph. 2:19).

In addition we have been made partakers of the divine

nature, have received the Spirit of adoption, and are heirs of God and joint heirs with Jesus Christ. Such a change of relationship cannot be brought about merely by the nominal desire of man nor by any normal design he may determine. Neither can it be obtained through natural descent nor secured by national decree (John 1:12).

Christ, as Heir of all things, is likewise King of kings, wherefore His righteous rule, and His regenerate race of mankind are in view in verse four of Psalm 87. "I will make mention of [Egypt] and Babylon to them that know Me: behold Philistia, and Tyre, with Ethiopia." Out from a world of materialistic imperialism and idolatry, corruption and confusion, as represented in Egypt and Babylon and from the three representative races of Shem, Japheth, and Ham, suggested in Philistia, Tyre, and Ethiopia, the Highest Himself emerges, emancipates, and entitles His people through regeneration to enter the city.

One faultless man arises from the ranks of humanity in the sphere of humiliation and takes by moral right the supreme station of honor in the realm of infinite holiness, there to be revealed in His true character, the Highest Himself. "Now that He ascended, what is it but that He also descended first into the lower parts of the earth? He that descended is the same also that ascended up far above all heavens, that He might fill all things" (Eph. 4:9-10). From the lowliest position He assumed on earth, our beloved Saviour rose to fill the loftiest place conceivable, which is described as above all heavens. Therefore, in dignity of disposition as well as in degree of dominion He exceeds every rank of renown, excels every position of prominence, and eclipses every superior station of might and majesty.

Although enthroned in unrivaled honor in those unrevealed heights, yet the tender compassions of His pity fail not, and the tokens of His faithfulness are strewn about us anew every morning. Even though He is environed in the unapproachable splendor of an undisclosed glory, and sways the scepter of supreme command and extreme control, yet His kindly sympathy and kingly strength sustain His people and see to their protection day by day.

In the light of such exalted Lordship, the repleteness of Christ's riches and resources cannot be estimated. No evident barriers can possibly hinder His beneficent bountifulness. No means of measurement can define His limitless loveliness, and no far-seeing telescope can bring into visibility the coastline of His shoreless supplies.

The vastness of His power is portrayed in a panorama of ponderous planets, the greatness of His might is manifested in the magnitude of the majestic mountains with their manifold minerals, while the immensity of His infinite strength is indicated in the star-strewn spaces of the heavens. No wonder that during His earthly ministry He spoke with a remarkable eloquence wholly free of extremes and extravagances. How could One who is Heir of all things, the very Prince of kings, whose rights are in the Heaven of heavens, ever overstate a claim? Is the declaration He made, "All that are in the graves shall hear My voice and shall come forth," an exaggeration? Is the statement He made to Caiaphas, the obdurate opposer, "Nevertheless I say unto you, hereafter shall ye see the Son of man sitting on the right hand of power and coming in the clouds of heaven," merely the excogitation of an excited mind? Nay, these are but minor expressions of the boundless power of Him who is the Highest Himself. So then we may confidently say, the potentialities of Christ are unpredictable, the prerogatives of Christ are unpronounceable, and the purposes of Christ are unpreventable.

THE HOLY ONE AND JUST

> But ye denied the Holy One and the Just, and desired a murderer to be granted unto you; And killed the Prince of life, whom God hath raised from the dead; whereof we are witnesses (Acts 3:14-15).

The whole narrative of this chapter centers in the worthiness and work of Christ, whose name and fame comprise the absorbing theme as set in relation to a man born lame. The preceding and succeeding chapters deal with the mighty movements of Pentecost, but the same power that wrought on multitudes was necessary to transform in the case of a single individual.

How fervently Peter directs the focus of attention away from himself and his fellow worker to Christ. "Why look ye so earnestly on us, as though by our own power or holiness we had made this man to walk? . . . the God of our fathers hath glorified His Son Jesus; whom ye delivered up, and denied Him in the presence of Pilate" (Acts 3:12-13). Without hesitancy or apology the apostle attributes the tremendous activities that were taking place day after day to the Holy One and Just.

Upon the basis of that holiness, he stresses the all-important need for repentance (verse 19). How despicable our ruined condition appears in the light of His perfect character of absolute holiness. No wonder that the soul that is smitten with a sense of guilt cries out for suitable and available mediation. What a discovery we make when we realize, "There is *one* God, and *one* mediator between God and men, the man Christ Jesus," and that this *one* Mediator is none other than the Holy *One* and Just, who in His omnipotence met this lame man in his impotence.

"A mediator is not a mediator of *one*, but God is *one*" (Gal. 3:20). This statement in the light of John 17:21-23 is a proclamation of Christ's deity, while 1 Timothy 2:5 presents His humanity. He is holy in both Godhead and manhood, and as Mediator He is always accessible, always available, and always amiable.

The purpose of His mediation is not to inflict penalty but to impart pardon and inaugurate preservation. He has made deliverance possible for every degree of wretchedness, willfulness, and weakness, no matter how dire or distant may be the dissimilarity, disability, and depravity. Christ not only erases the guilt but endows with grace, energizes with power, and enriches the emancipated life with the beauties of virtue. As a Mediator He listens lovingly for the voice of prayer and praise and lavishes freely His gifts of mercy on all that seek His face. In fulfilling this great and generous function He is forever enduringly strong, entirely sincere, and eternally steadfast.

The main emphasis in the passages quoted rests on the little word *one*. We can scarcely conceive of any other word used in Scripture in relation to Godhead that has greater significance. In connection with the fact of one Spirit, one Lord and "*one* God and Father of all who is above all and through all and in all," *one* is used in the chapter ten times. In Matthew 18 where Christ stressed the importance of *one* He used the word a dozen times. When Paul the apostle is dealing with one Spirit and one body in his message to Corinth, he uses *one* sixteen times in the presentation (1 Cor. 12). On the occasion whent the instructions were given to Moses concerning one taber-nacle (Ex. 26:6), *one* occurs twenty-four times in the chapter. At the time of the dedication of the altar in the tabernacle, when Moses heard the voice of *One* speaking unto him off the mercy-seat (Num. 7:89), *one* is used in the chapter eighty-six times.

The significance of the word *one* in relation to Christ is that, in both primacy and precedency and as the Holy One, He stands in priority to all others, and in His preeminence He sur-passes all. *One* also suggests sovereignty and betokens a superiority that supersedes every other expression of holiness. Then again *one* is the hallmark of infinity and the seal of in-dependency, expressing at the same time the entity of His per-son and the eternity of His priesthood. In Christ we meet with harmony united with humility, and the one of simplicity is linked with the one of sublimity. Herein we are introduced to the unity and unanimity of Godhead, "Hear, O Israel: The LORD our God is one LORD" (Deut. 6:4). The word *one* in this case is a compound unity. Maimonides, who was educated under the Saracen regime, substituted the Arabic word, which is an absolute singular, and virtually turned the Jewish mind to unitarianism. Spinoza the philosopher, Heine the poet, and others of his successors continued the use of the substitute, which destroys the outstanding fact of Old Testament revela-tion concerning the character of Godhead.

THE HOPE OF ISRAEL

O the hope of Israel, the Saviour thereof in time of trouble, why shouldest Thou be as a stranger in the land? . . . O LORD, the hope of Israel, all that forsake Thee shall be ashamed, and they that depart from Me shall be written in the earth, because they have forsaken the LORD, the fountain of living waters (Jer. 14:8; 17:13).

Because that for the hope of Israel I am bound with this chain (Acts 28:20).

The Hope of Israel is definitely a title of Messiah. It is related to the kingdom of God and the salvation of God as predicted by the prophets and preached by Paul (Acts 26:6-8). On account of this very testimony Paul was apprehended by the Jews and arraigned before the governors of the land. "And now I stand and am judged for the *hope* of the promise made of God unto our fathers: Unto which promise our twelve tribes, instantly serving God day and night, *hope* to come. For which *hope's* sake, king Agrippa, I am accused of the Jews. Why should it be thought a thing incredible with you, that God should raise the dead?"

The dignified, descriptive declaration of Paul's defense before King Agrippa is one of the finest pieces of oratory in all literature. He did not contend with the Jews over their false charge of sedition, but confined his statement to the superlative subject of salvation. He courageously and capably affirmed that the reconciling death and victorious resurrection of Christ fulfilled the predictions of prophets and the pledges of the promises made to the Fathers. This was the apostle's constant theme (see Rom. 15:8-13). He did not modify or qualify the fact at any time, but affirmed it clearly and confidently. The resurrection from the dead is bound up inextricably with the Hope of Israel and is affirmed by Abraham, Job, Moses, David, Isaiah, Daniel, Hosea, and others of the prophets. Messiah himself avowed, "I am the resurrection and the life." In the light of the almighty omnipotent God, resurrection from the dead is not incredible but inevitable, for He has pledged it, and one word from the Lord God outweighs in worth and wisdom a whole library of human utterances.

The arresting grandeur of Christ's monumental mastery over death, the momentous marvel of His resurrection, and the matchless miracle of His ascension, dim into insignificance all former events in history.

Scientists may speak of a general resurrection as being a grave difficulty, but the word *difficulty* is not in the dictionary of Deity, nor is impossibility in the vocabulary of the victorious and infinite Christ. We do not flout human science nor do we fear it, but we favor a much higher fount of authority. If the present radio and recording system had been described in a university a century ago, it would have been declared preposterous. When Paul the apostle introduced this subject of the Hope of Israel, he raised eternal issues that were universal in their then present application. In the wonderful message of Romans 15 Paul declares in verses 8 and 9: "Jesus Christ was a minister of the circumcision for the truth of God, to confirm the promises made unto the fathers: And that the Gentiles might glorify God for His mercy."

The promises of God are supported and sustained by wisdom's seven pillars (Prov. 9:1).

1. God's superiority and sovereignty will not allow Him to withhold mercy or mediation from any one people (Ps. 145:9; Is. 55:7).
2. His power and preeminence will not permit Him to fail or falter in a single pledge He has made (Josh. 23:14).
3. His justice and prudence will not allow Him to deceive or despise one solitary soul (Job 34:12; 36:5).
4. His grace and goodness will not allow Him to forget or forsake any individual creature anywhere (Ezek. 18:4; Is. 49:15).
5. His truth and tenderness will not permit Him to change or countermand one syllable of His covenant (2 Sam. 23:5; Jer. 31:33-35; Luke 1:68-72).
6. His glory and greatness will not allow Him to deflect or defer one proffered signal of help (Heb. 13:6).
7. His fatherhood and faithfulness will not permit Him to disregard or discard an atom of assurance promised to the believing soul (Gal. 3:15-21; 2 Cor. 1:20).

Notice that the word *promise* occurs seven times in Galatians; three, in the space of as many verses; which pertains to the covenant confirmed before of God in Christ (verse 17). This covers the widest range (Gal. 3:27-29; see also Eph. 1:9-10). "Behold, Thou hast made the heaven and the earth . . . there is nothing too hard for Thee" (Jer. 32:17). "Behold, I am the LORD, the God of all flesh: is there any thing too hard for Me?" (Jer. 32:27) In addition to faith in the promises, the believer enjoys the blessed anchorage of hope in the eternal purpose which preceded all the differences of nation, race, class, creed, and sex.

THE HEAD OF THE CHURCH

And He is the head of the body, the church: who is the beginning, the firstborn from the dead (Col. 1:18).

We should rejoice exultingly in the glorious fact that our Lord and Saviour Jesus Christ holds every office of supreme headship in creation, revelation, redemption, reconciliation, and regeneration. His immutable will and immortal wisdom are qualifications that are not found in the character of any other administrator. No one else has the insight and integrity, the dignity and durability of Christ to fill these supreme stations of high office. The memorable splendor attending His earthly manifestation was a mark of the magnitude of merit and measure of might lying behind His marvelous mission and the mystery of His passion. Little wonder that the hosts on high ascribe to Him power, riches, wisdom, strength, honor, glory, and blessing for ever and ever (Rev. 5:12-13).

The position Christ occupies in headship is wholly independent of earthly empires. "The stone which the builders rejected is become the head of the corner: This was the Lord's doing, and it is marvelous in our eyes" (Mark 12:10-11). Wherefore His precedence, prominence, prescience, and permanence are not honors derived, or capabilities conferred, but with these as a background He came into the world voluntarily to secure honor and headship of a totally new kind on the basis of personal sacrifice and perfect devotion in service.

As Creator, He is the head of every man (1 Cor. 11:3), but by consent He came to earth to become Head of the Body, the Church; therefore this position of preeminence is not derived from any source of natural descent or national distinction. No church existed until He founded it, prepared for its construction, and purchased the material for this new social order, and built the same into a habitation of fellowship.

The relationship of Christ as "head over all things to the church, Which is His body," expresses "the fulness of Him that filleth all in all" (Eph. 1:20-23). Here again the essential fullness of Christ, who is the fullness of Godhead bodily (Col. 1:15), is adorned and amplified by an acquired fullness in the Church. The plenitude of the one has a new magnitude added as an adornment on the ground of reconciliation. Twelve figures are used to express the breadth and beauty of this secured fullness of which Christ is Head.

1. When the Church is figured as a family, Christ is the Firstborn, a title of relationship that introduces His superiority and precedence. His likeness is impressed on the myriad members of the Christian household of faith.
2. When the Church is featured as a flock, Christ is the Chief Shepherd, an official capacity that expresses the sympathy and sufficiency of His superintendence in guidance and guardianship.
3. In the case of church society being viewed as a fellowship, Christ is the bond of peace that binds together and the basis of brotherhood that unites for cooperation in worship and witness.
4. If the Church is considered as a spotless Bride, Christ is the faultless Bridegroom, manifesting and maintaining superlative love in steadfast fidelity and faithfulness.
5. If we contemplate the Church as a body, Christ is the sole Head, organizing every function and overseeing every facility, thus displaying His supernatural and omniscient mind.
6. The Church as a building brings into clear light the fact of Christ as the Foundation who frames and fashions living stones in order to build a spiritual temple for the habitation of God. "Ye are His workmanship." This

aspect demonstrates the superseding wisdom of His plan and purpose.

7. The Church in militant array as a battalion in conflict against the powers of darkness, makes room for the unveiling of Christ as Captain in His superexcellent leadership and lordship, directing the campaigns of the centuries against evil forces.

8. The function of the Church in her fruitbearing is likened to the branches of the Vine. Christ is the True Vine, supplying the vitality and the virtue for bearing much fruit, through the medium of His superabounding grace.

9. Our Lord is likewise the Creator of the one new man, which presents the Church in her character as the Custodian of the truth of the gospel, to declare and demonstrate the righteousness of God.

10. The Church as a gathering in the unity of the Spirit, in the face of all the disparity and diversity that exists, confirms the supervising authority of Christ in Heaven and on earth, and His ability to summon and sustain an innumerable host, to conform them to His own image and to cause them to abide in unity and amity for ever.

11. The Church, when considered as a priesthood, functions under the headship of Christ, the great High Priest who in His supervision secures and safeguards every sacred sanction of the sanctuary where spiritual sacrifices are offered and spiritual blessings are enjoyed.

12. In yet another figure, the inheritance of the saints in light depicts the Church as those who are heirs of God and joint heirs with Christ the Son, who is Heir of all in His superposition, controlling the riches of grace and glory.

These unsearchable riches of Christ are stupendous in their magnitude and magnificence, and set forth the immeasurability and inexhaustibility of the headship He so rightly holds. As Head of the Body, the Church, He is the beginning, the Firstborn from the dead, that in all things He might have the preeminence (Col. 1:18).

In this chief center of celestial control, Christ administers the power to promote His own interests, the prerogatives to answer prayer, and the providences that assure provision for

His people. When we consider the myriads to whom He ministers, which include all the saintly scholars, wise counselors, prominent leaders, eminent expositors, true teachers, excellent evangelists, sympathetic shepherds, missionaries of merit, tireless translators, worthy workers, memorable martyrs, and the hosts which make up the innumerable multitude, how wonderful Christ must be, to be Head of such a tremendous concourse of saints!

The headship of Christ is immortally graceful, imperially powerful, and impartially merciful. His dignity is associated with renowned majesty and ageless maturity, so that He far outdates the history of humanity and outvies the longevity of the most honored in leadership.

THE HEIFER WITHOUT BLEMISH

> Bring thee a red heifer without spot, wherein is no blemish, and upon which never came yoke. And ye shall give her unto Eleazar the priest, that he may bring her forth without the camp, and one shall slay her before his face (Num. 19:2-3).

How unique and unrivaled Christ appears in His many-sided character, with unbounded qualifications and unlimited abilities; all of which He harnesses and utilizes for the good of man and the glory of God.

By virtue of the vast depths of His deity and the eternal merits of Calvary, with its sacrificial passion, He established an enduring fountain of cleansing for all the defilements contracted from dead works. The whole of Numbers 19 introduces the perpetual provision for purification which Christ procured on behalf of His people, so that the sacred sanctions of communion with God may be maintained.

These types of holier spiritual verities are not as some imagine, dark mysteries to bewilder the mind, but clearly defined illustrations for declaring the weightier values of divine truth.

Four features are described as being necessary before the red heifer could be selected as suitable for sacrifice. These are extremely important in view of the divine nature of the great antitype which they foreshadowed.

The first feature is "without spot," indicating the comeliness of Christ, who is "without sin" (Heb. 4:15); secondly, "wherein is no blemish," introducing the character of Christ, "who knew no sin" (2 Cor. 5:21); thirdly, "whereon never came yoke," intimating the conduct of Christ, "who did no sin" (1 Pet. 2:22); fourthly, "slain without the camp," implying the conformity of Christ to the will of God, "in Him is no sin" (1 John 3:5). "I," said He, "do always those things that please Him." No stain defiled His soul, no pollution tainted His life, no blemish marred His purity and no spot tarnished His sanctity. His was holiness in the highest degree, His pureness expressed perfect character, for God could not accept an offering short of such standards. "It shall be perfect to be accepted; there shall be no blemish therein" (Lev. 22:21).

We are fully aware that communion with God may be enriched and enhanced by conformity to His will, but intentional willfulness or inadvertent weakness mar the enjoyment of this precious privilege.

To meet the need, God ordained a priesthood to offset the iniquity of the one (Num. 18), and ordered an offering to overcome the inability of the other (Num. 19). Paul the apostle enlarges on the weaknesses of a quickened soul in Romans 7, a chapter which closes with a heartfelt need: "O wretched man that I am! who shall deliver me from the body of this *death?*" (Rom. 7:24) Notice that death is the cause of the defilements in the section we are considering. A similar confirmation is given in Hebrews: "For if the blood of bulls and of goats, and the ashes of a heifer sprinkling the unclean, sanctifieth to the purifying of the flesh; How much more shall the blood of Christ, who through the eternal Spirit offered Himself without spot to God, purge your conscience from *dead* works to serve the living God?" (Heb. 9:13-14)

In the ceremony connected with the red heifer offering, the limbs of the cedar tree were entwined with hyssop and then wholly covered with scarlet before being put into the fire. The counterpart of this symbolism was expressed in the manifestation. The majesty of Christ was entwined with the meekness of His humility and clothed upon with the dignity of His personal authority, as representing God manifest in the flesh. His loftiness was cedar-like, His lowliness was as the hyssop, while His loveliness was likened to the beauty of scarlet. The entireness of His essential excellence went into the fire to answer for our frailties. Therefore we not only obtain justification in Christ, but a complete store of merit reposes in Him which procures purification from daily defilements.

No one is more preciously lovable and inexpressibly desirable than Christ. Among the countless blessings of His covenant, this benefit of banishing our defilements in order to maintain us in communion is inestimable. The beautiful figure signified in the heifer suggests the wonderful compassion Christ expresses toward us in our mortal infirmities. What fullness flows in His divine compassion, which includes the gentleness of His grace, the considerateness of His care, the sweetness of His mercy, and the tenderness of His love. He secures and safeguards the relationship, for if we as enemies were reconciled by His death, much more being reconciled we shall be saved by His life (Rom. 5:10). What He has already done assures us that He will continue to maintain. The genial waters for our cleansing leap from the crystal spring of His inner perfection. Peter had been to the laver of regeneration, but he needed the daily purification of life if he was to continue in cooperation and communion with His Lord. "Jesus saith to him, He that is washed needeth not save to wash his feet, but is clean every whit" (John 13:10).

> "Clean every whit," Thou saidst it, Lord;
> 　Shall one suspicion lurk?
> Thine surely is a faithful word
> 　And Thine a finished work.

Maimonides wrote in the thirteenth century that throughout Israel's national history nine heifers were offered in connection with this ceremony and that Messiah would offer the tenth. Messiah has already fulfilled the entire symbolism of the offering and the river of the water of life, clear as crystal, now flows from the throne of God.

THE HEALER OF MEN

I am the LORD that healeth thee. . . . When the even was
come, they brought unto Him many that were possessed with
devils: and He cast out the spirits with His word, and healed all
that were sick (Ex. 15:26; Matt. 8:16).

In reviewing life, golden hours appear few and transient,
and their replacement with grief-torn conditions plunges us
into the throes of trial. However, we are never deserted when
we encounter such ordeals, but we are able to turn to the
fadeless light of His changeless countenance and solicit from
our unfailing Friend grace to help in time of need. The healing of His seamless dress and the loving help of His tireless
hands are "by our beds of pain; we touch Him in life's storm
and stress and we are whole again." Chastening is common to
all the children of God, yet withal it should be a cheer and
comfort, "for whom the Lord loveth He chasteneth" (Heb.
12:6).

Who is unfamiliar with the tornado and the tempest? Who
among us has never entered a wilderness or encountered a
winter? Who, may we ask, has never experienced nausea or
endured a trying night? These are common matter-of-fact
circumstances that exert a very definite ministry in the lives of
us all. The turbulent tornado and tempestuous storm help us
to appreciate the deeper values of the prophetic message:
"Behold, a King shall reign in righteousness . . . And a man
shall be as a hiding place from the wind, and a covert from the
tempest" (Is. 32:1-2). Isaiah said earlier that the overflowing
scourge was to pass through the land (28:15), so it is a good
thing to know of the refuge in the rock of ages (26:4). The
pressure of circumstances signified by the wind, and the
perilous conditions of the tempest are sure to come our way
sooner or later.

In the tempest of terrors on Galilee, the disciples experienced the thrill of wonder and worship. Their souls were gripped by the spectacle of the Son of Man controlling the wind
and calming the waves. Henceforth they could tell forth His
mastery over material forces. A tempestuous storm at sea

brings some men to their senses; a serious loss in business has caused distress in other minds. Such have been driven to seek the more substantial riches, and have proved that godliness yields profits more durable than bank securities. The wilderness with its solitariness, so streamless and shapeless as it is, wrought havoc among the multitude in exposing the willfulness and weakness of mortal man, and the wretchedness and waywardness of the human heart; but it also brought into clear light the wisdom of the divine plan and purpose, and the wealth of the divine patience and provision. He still allures into the wilderness in order to fulfill His ministry of comfort and hope (Hos. 2:14-15).

Winter with its cold reverses and chilly blasts provides a suitable atmosphere for the crystal snowflakes that garnish the landscape and hide all scars. If it were not for the icy cold, no fleecy whiteness would mantle the landscape and glisten in the light. But for winter, the fruit trees would miss their rest and cease production, and the wheatfields would lose their vitality and fail to furnish the prolific crops. So likewise His chastening hand causes real heartsearching, and yieldeth "the peaceable fruit of righteousness unto them which are exercised thereby" (Heb. 12:11).

Nausea nullifies our taste and curbs the appetite for natural indulgences, and halts our hankering after showy and sensual things. Sickness usually furnishes us with more time for consideration, so that spiritual realities and eternal verities may claim our attention. Sickness has an eloquence that is hard to silence, and combines with sorrow to supply two handmaidens for furthering the Saviour's ministry of evangelism. "Before I was afflicted I went astray: but now have I kept Thy word. . . . It is good for me that I have been afflicted; that I might learn Thy statutes" (Ps. 119:67,71).

Night shows a neighborly friendliness to the stars, for apart from darkness we would not see the scintillating glories of the heavenly bodies and would miss the myriad marvels twinkling in calm serenity like jewels in the sky. The magnificence of the celestial beauties of Pleiades and Orion, Alpha Centauri and Omega Centauri, the Beta and Gamma Lyrae, the bright star Deneb of the constellation of Cygnus, the bright star Sirius, or the brightest of all Venus — the magnificence of these would be virtually unknown but for the night. Why does the One who creates such marvels consider man at all? (Ps. 8:4)

Trials touch the most vital interests of our lives, but at the same time they bring vividly to light the holy presence of the Healer and the assurance of His help. Not until the bitterness of Marah had blackened the prospects of any betterment did the Lord order Moses to cut down the tree that reversed the dilemma and turned bitterness to sweetness and distress to delight. The crucibles for refinement change, but the controlling hand of the Refiner that remolds and remakes is ever constant to console and compensate. We may not expect to encounter bitterness in the path of obedience to God, but Abraham ran into famine when he obeyed (Gen. 12) and the nation faced the difficulty of no water when following the Lord (Ex. 12). Yet He always has the antidote for our ailments at hand. "Bless the LORD, O my soul . . . who healeth all thy diseases; Who redeemeth Thy life from destruction; who crowneth thee with loving-kindness and tender mercies" (Ps. 103:2-4).

THE HIGHWAY OF LIFE

And a highway shall be there, and a way, and it shall be called The way of holiness. . . . And the ransomed of the LORD shall return, and come to Zion with songs and everlasting joy upon their heads (Is. 35:8,10).

The eternal gloom and doom of Idumea described in chapter 34 stands in striking contrast with the everlasting gladness and delight of Zion. Many roads lead to ruination but there is only one Highway of Holiness that leads Heavenward, homeward, and Godward. Chapter 35 is studded with a select group of the very choicest words such as blossom, springs, excellency, glory, singing, joy, rejoicing, and such like, betokening the new tone and transformation to be instituted by Messiah. The transactions recorded were certainly not realized when the captives returned from banishment in Babylon. The secret of this amazing change is definitely stated.

"Behold, your God will come . . . He will come and save you" (verse 4). Isaiah the prophet repeats this radiant message on the occasion when the Lord destroys the veil spread over all nations and swallows up death in victory: "Lo, this is our God; we have waited for Him, and He will save us: this is the LORD; we have waited for Him, we will be glad and rejoice in His salvation" (Is. 25:9). Paul the apostle quotes from this portion when speaking of the rapture (1 Cor. 15:54). Isaiah again says, in connection with the coming of the great Shepherd heralded by the voice of one crying in the wilderness: "Behold, the Lord GOD will come with strong hand, and His arm shall rule for Him: behold, His reward is with Him. . . . He shall gather the lambs with His arm, and carry them in His bosom" (Is. 40:10-11).

In chapter 35 the harassing wilderness and haphazard wanderings of life are things of the past, for a new Highway, yea a Holyway opens before the pilgrim host. The only way to the God of holiness must needs be a holy way. The miracles of might and mercy mentioned in verses five and six were wrought by Messiah during His manifestation and He declared "I am the way," which proves the validity of His claim as Regenerator and Saviour.

We are introduced to four types of bodily infirmity and physical incapacity to indicate the state of mankind prior to the Highway being introduced. These are classified as the blind, deaf, lame, and dumb. What chance have they of determining a way to God?

Blindness, which is defect in perception, expresses an incapacity which affects the power of obtaining knowledge. Christ used the figure in this relation in John 9:41. (See also Is. 6:9-10.) Deafness is a deficiency in hearing, which affects the understanding. Lameness is a defect that hampers activity and affects the powers of motion. Dumbness prevents speech, and stands for complete incapacity of utterance.

The miraculous change affected in these physical maladies points to the greater spiritual marvels wrought by the divine power of regeneration. Christ the Regenerator re-establishes the sight capacity for the acquiring of knowledge.

"Except a man be born again, he cannot *see* the kingdom of God" (John 3:3). Christ the Revealer reinstates the hearing capacity for understanding. "Then opened He their understanding, that they might understand the scriptures" (Luke 24:45). Christ the Restorer reimplants the strength to walk, which is capability of action. "Jesus saith unto him, Rise, take up thy bed, and walk. And immediately the man was made whole, and took up his bed, and walked" (John 5:8-9). Christ the Ransomer recovers the faculty of speech, the competency of utterance for praise and proclamation. "Behold, they brought to Him a dumb man possessed with a devil. And when the devil was cast out, the dumb spake: and the multitudes marveled" (Mat. 9:32-33).

Eternal principles are involved in these matters; therefore, if there is to be a highway by which the four classes represented are to wend their way to God, that way can only be through Him who remolds, reclaims, remakes, and reconciles. Wherefore He proclaimed it in the ears of all the world and all its generations: "I am the way, the truth, and the life: no man cometh unto the Father, but by Me" (John 14:6). No one is fit to approach the Father without Him. Justice must be vindicated, debts must be liquidated, sin must be propitiated, and right of access substantiated. Christ achieves all this.

Much more that we must pass over is dealt with in the chapter, but one other feature requires notice. The four terms—*wilderness, desert, parched ground,* and *thirsty land*—are figures used for hindrances that hamper progress. All such opposition must be overthrown, all obstacles must be obliterated, all oppression must be overcome and all offenses must be ousted. In other words, the vanquished evils must be banished and the resisting factors removed. So here we find this is done. Frustrating factors have been replaced with facilities which are likened to waters, streams, pools, and springs. When our Lord Jesus Christ put into operation His omnipotent powers, all that was desirable was done; so the way of holiness was established forever. The wayfarers on this Highway are now travelers, not triflers.

THE HEIR OF ALL THINGS

God, who at sundry times and in divers manners spake in
time past unto the fathers by the prophets, hath in these last
days spoken unto us by His Son, whom He hath appointed heir
of all things, by whom also He made the worlds (Heb. 1:1-2).

But those husbandmen said among themselves, This is the
heir; come, let us kill Him, and the inheritance shall be ours
(Mark 12:7).

The adequacy of Christ's power in kingship and the
supremacy of His position in lordship are completed by the
universality of His possession in heirship. The special feature
of His title to the entire inheritance as Son of God (Mark 1:1),
and His superior right of claim to all humanity is clearly expressed in the Gospel of Mark (see 12:6-11).

In this message the earthly aspect of the great estate is portrayed as overrun by a usurper who works his havoc through a
fourfold method of domination. These destroying factors may
be stated as the disruption of sin, the dislocation of nations,
disease, and death (Mark 16:17-18).

Christ the Heir was manifested and appeared in the midst of
the estate as the Kinsman-Redeemer. He was purposely sent,
according to His own teaching, to recover the rent due from
those who had been sanctioned the lease. Palestine itself was a
miniature picture of the great enactment. All cropping lands
were leased for fifty-year periods, and at the end of each term
the year of jubilee was celebrated. The trumpet of jubilee was
sounded on the tenth day of the seventh month, which was the
great day of the atonement, and the celebration that followed
was the occasion for the acknowledgment of God as being the
Proprietor of the whole land (Lev. 25:23). "The land shall not
be sold for ever, the land is Mine." Psalm 8 should be read in
conjunction with this outlook, also Psalm 24. Without the propitiation of atonement there was no liberation (Lev. 25:9-10).
Without redemption for the land there was no possession (Lev.
25:24-27). Without substitution for sin there was no celebration. "In the day of atonement shall ye make the trumpet

sound throughout all your land. . . . It shall be a jubilee unto you" (Lev. 25:9-10).

The great counterpart of this legislation is depicted in the final unveiling, in which book the Heir of all things is described and displayed in all the perfection of His wondrous person and vocation, exercising His sovereign authority and superior prerogatives.

Following the astounding celebration of a universally realized redemption, at which ceremony Christ takes hold of the title deeds bearing the seven authentic seals of the celestial court (Rev. 5), the final hour arrives when the seventh trumpet sounds and the kingdom of the world becomes His and He reigns forever and ever (Rev. 11:15). This is the most far-reaching transaction, described in writing, that was ever concluded in connection with the claims of heirship, and determines forever the rightful ownership of Christ to all things. No future legislation in any court can refute the legality of the verdict or disannul the decision determined. The measure and magnitude of the Lord's majesty in His capacity as Heir of all things is indescribable. What wisdom and worthiness, wealth and worship rightfully belong to Him! We should also revel in the fact that "The Spirit itself beareth witness with our spirit, that we are the children of God: And if children, then heirs; heirs of God, and joint-heirs with Christ" (Rom. 8:16).

Peter reminds us that the inheritance is incorruptible, undefiled, and never fades away (1 Pet. 1:4).

THE HELPER OF THE NEEDY

For He hath said, I will never leave thee nor forsake thee. So that we may boldly say, The Lord is my helper, and I will not fear what man shall do unto me (Heb. 13:5-6).

What the Lord has said induces His loved ones to speak. He said, "I will never leave thee"; so I say, "The Lord is my helper." This is indisputable logic. An immortal splendor shines out from the steadfast sayings of our sovereign Saviour, who is also the great Shepherd of the sheep, and forever beyond the reach of death (verse 20). How genuine is His guardianship as He guides His flock. How constant is His care as He considers His family. How faithful is His fellowship in favoring His friends with an abiding assurance of His presence. His pledge is more lasting in value than all the treasure in the vaults of the world's banks. Christ's will is immutable and He has determined never to leave nor forsake me. He made many memorable promises to Abraham, Joseph, Moses, and David and fulfilled them. Joshua also was able to say to Israel at the close of his famous career, "Not one thing hath failed of all the good things which the LORD your God spake concerning you; all are come to pass unto you, and not one thing hath failed" (Josh. 23:14).

An ever-enduring charm characterizes the constancy of Christ's pledges and promises. He said in all certitude to His disciples, "Heaven and earth shall pass away, but My words shall not pass away" (Matt. 24:35).

A thousand times blessed is His promise to befriend us; it forms a foundation for restful confidence, furnishes a fountain of refreshing cheer, and fashions a fortress for resolute courage.

In the light of what He has said, let each one of us say, "The Lord is my helper. . . . I will not fear what man shall do unto me." Think of it! The help of this almighty, ever-abiding, omnipotent Friend is actually mine. Pause for a moment and contemplate the revealed record of this dignified Companion in this very book of Hebrews. He is superior to angels and patriarchs in chapters 1 and 2. He is statelier than apostles and prophets in chapters 3 and 4, and saintlier than Aaron and the priesthood in 5 and 7. He is far more sublime in His functions and vocations than all other altars and patterns in 8 to 10, and much more supreme in renown and resoluteness than all other authors and pioneers in 11 and 12.

Imagine if you will His immortal strength, inscrutable might, and infinite power being compacted together to render the help necessary to the people of God. Is this conceivable that with all His knowledge as the Lord of legislators, with all His kingliness as the Lord of leaders, with all His kindliness as the Lord of lovers, the very Lord of lords Himself should be my Helper? The enemy may suggest that we speak it in a whisper,

nay verily we may boldly say, "The Lord is my helper."
Remember also, He is without variableness. This fact is immediately stated: "Jesus Christ, the same yesterday, and to
day, and for ever" (13:8). Herein lies the most sacred source of
our comfort and cheer.

Half a century ago in the art gallery of Glasgow there hung
a striking picture for public inspection which the artist had
titled "Help." The scene depicted a massive cliff in the
background with a large cave. The ruggedness of the jutting
rocks at the mouth of the cavern and the dense darkness within
made it appear to be the lair of some terrifying monster.
Standing in front of the entrance was a wee lad with a terror-
stricken face. Beside him stood his big manly brother, who was
holding the child's hand and looking intently into his face, as
much as to say, "Do not be afraid of anything that may be in
that cavern, for I am with you, I have hold of your hand, and
will prevent anything that may come out of there from hurting
you." The three syllables of the word used by Martha
beautifully express these features of companionship: *sun,*
with; *anti,* in the stead of; *lambano,* to hold the hand: *sunan-*
tilambanomai. The request Martha made to the Master implies, "Bid her be with me, and act for me as one holding my
hand."

THE HE GOAT

An he goat also; and a king, against whom there is no rising
up (Prov. 30:31).

The goat is referred to on one hundred twenty-six occasions
in the Old Testament. It played a very important part in the
sacrificial system of Israel. The suitability of the goat as a symbol of an offering lay in its strength and surefootedness. The
goat never slips no matter how steep the rock or narrow the
ledge. Our Saviour never slipped in word, thought, or act.
Therefore He offered Himself without spot to God. The importance of the goat may be impressed by the fact that one of
the presents brought by the Arabians to King Jehoshaphat included seven thousand seven hundred he goats (2 Chron.
17:11).

The chapter in Scripture which supplies one of the most complete pictures of Christ's substitutionary work is in the book of Leviticus; on the occasion referred to, two goats were prominent in the ceremony (Lev. 16:5).

One of these animals stood as a figure of propitiation, and it was slain to meet the requirements of justice. The other was a symbol of substitution, and priestly hands were laid upon it, and confession made of the sins of the nation before it was dispatched into the wilderness. We should remember that God in His character and nature is essentially, entirely, and eternally holy. Humanity has nothing in common with holiness and is therefore excluded from the divine presence. Man stands in need of a meritorious Mediator to undertake his cause. In this piece of ritual God signified how approach could be made. The figures reflect a great reality and are shadows of a sublime substance, which is Christ. Only through a representative Redeemer and Reconciler may man approach God in righteousness; therefore He has appointed that such access must be through reconciliation which is followed by an assured acceptance in the Beloved.

We are entirely dependent on the efficacy of Christ's perfect sacrifice of Himself. The stipulation was made in the law of offerings, "It shall be perfect to be accepted." This feature was of the highest importance. None of us is unblemished in mind, motive, and merit, so that no man can by any means redeem his brother. All are imperfect; "there is none righteous, no not one."

Because our Lord has achieved a perfect reconciliation, God can irrevocably forgive the sinner who seeks His mercy. To be accepted in Christ means that sin has been vanquished and has vanished, for we are justified. The burden of sin has been effectually and completely transferred to Christ, and He has eternally and finally answered for it. "By his own blood He entered in once into the holy place, having obtained eternal redemption for us" (Heb. 9:12).

We should not omit the means that were ordained in the tabernacle ceremony to set forth the exclusive excellence of the true Substance, Christ, as a perfect and acceptable sacrifice.

Associated with the offering were vessels of purest gold, incense of sweetest perfume, robes of rarest beauty, jewels of greatest value, curtains of choicest fabrics, light of brightest radiance, and cherubim of highest significance. Amid the sacredness of these costly surroundings the crimson sign of a completed sacrifice could be clearly seen, for the blood of the goat as the sin offering of the people was sprinkled seven times upon the mercy seat, and before it (Lev. 16:15; compare verse 14). This feature was repeated at the brazen altar (verses 18-19). The suggestiveness of this in relation to the blood of Christ would carry us beyond our scope, so we shall be content with a bare reference to the parallel in the New Testament.

The blood of Christ procures redemption (Eph. 1:7; 1 Pet. 1:18-19); promotes peace (Col. 1:20); purifies from sin (1 John 1:7); provides access (Heb. 10:19); pledges fellowship (1 Cor. 10:16-17); proclaims justification (Rom. 5:9); and proffers victory (Rev. 12:11). This constitutes the perfect presentation of the blood of Christ before God, for our assurance, acceptance, and association. Let us repair often to the Cross and view afresh His crucifixion which preceded His coronation, for memory is the soul's best monitor to minister the message of Christ's sacrificial love to the heart. Thereby we shall be maintained in the warmth of affection and wonder of worship toward the Saviour, combined with loyal service, which are the salutary fruits of gratitude.

THE HIGH PRIEST FOREVER

Within the veil; Whither the forerunner is for us entered, even Jesus, made an high priest for ever after the order of Melchisedec (Heb. 6:19-20).

The prominent characters of the Old Testament are described graphically with the definite object in view of directing our attention to Christ the magnificent. As High Priest, our Lord is greater than Aaron, who held office temporarily, and is declared to be after the order of Melchisedec, a priest of perpetuity who had neither beginning of days nor end of life. Wherefore Christ is first and foremost in this sacred office. His priestly mediation precedes, surpasses, and supercedes all other mediation for He has no superior or successor. In His consecration to this sacred service He wore the miter of holiness, the girdle of truth, the breastplate of righteousness, the radiant robe of glory and beauty, the garment of praise, and the epaulets of Urim and Thummim which expressed the lights and perfections of Deity (Ex. 28:30). The fragrance of the holy anointing oil suggested the transcendent excellence of His perfect character, while His full hands of sweet incense which flooded the sanctuary with rich odors set forth His faultless conduct. In reality His virtue exceeded His vesture, His royalty excelled His robes, His grace outvied His garments, and His attributes surpassed His attire.

The dignified comeliness and majestic beauty of Christ's priestly service consist in its perpetuity: "He ever liveth to make intercession for [us]"; "wherefore He is able also to save them to the uttermost." He abides perpetually, knows us intimately, understands thoroughly, and undertakes perfectly.

> Say not, my soul, "Whence shall I find a priest who cares,
>   Changeless and patient, who every trial shares,
> Whose sympathy abides, whose love endures,
>   Who helpeth mortal frailty, and rest assures."
> For Christ Himself will act for thee in every need,
>   He ever liveth a glorious Priest indeed,
> All maintenance provides, upholds for sure;
>   He will present thee faultless, evermore secure.

In His representation Christ reveals God to man and represents man to God. Through Him reconciliation is available and association is the result, instead of the alienation that formerly existed. Localized shrines and temples are no longer necessary for access to the Father of mercies and God of all comfort. Christ displaced this means of approach and declared, "No man cometh unto the Father, but by Me" (John 14:6). His own perfect relationship and peerless righteousness assure to us both access and acceptance (Eph. 1:6; 1 John 2:2).

In His ministration, Christ is matchless as High Priest. The merits of His vocation as Mediator secured atonement for sin, and procured priceless spiritual gifts and moral graces for bestowment upon those redeemed and reconciled. Therefore, Christ has the prerogative to bestow these precious gifts upon His people as the Minister of the heavenly sanctuary (Heb. 8:1-3).

Some of the corporate gifts are enumerated in Ephesians 4:7-12, and a further list appears in 1 Corinthians 12:28-31. He is able to enrich with utterance, knowledge, grace, and every other requirement desirable for acceptable worship and effective service (1 Cor. 1:4-7). This High Priest has unlimited resources at His disposal and holds the exclusive right to dispense these riches to those who desire to obtain such. The personal gifts include the grace to beautify, the love to edify, the truth to sanctify, the power to qualify, the hope to purify, the joy to gratify, the peace to satisfy, and the praise to glorify His blessed name. How much more honoring it would be if we sought more earnestly and eagerly by prayer these spiritual treasures, instead of occupying our time with the trifles of physical necessities. Even Paul could say, "What have we that we have not received?"

In His intercession as High Priest our gracious Lord fulfills one of His most important features of service for the maintenance of His people. The accomplishment of redemption and the administration of the sanctuary is followed by advocacy for the saints: "We have an advocate with the Father, Jesus Christ the righteous." When we look back and recall the journey of Israel from Egypt to Canaan, with the trials of the wilderness, the temptations by the way, the tasks of burden-bearing, the troubles in the camp, the threats from enemies, and a score of other matters that challenged advance, where would they have been without priestly intercession? The Angel of His presence saved them (Isa. 63:9).

We likewise have a High Priest who is touched with feeling for our infirmities, who has compassion on the ignorant and them who are out of the way (Heb. 5:2).

How stupendous is the sacerdotal work of our all-superior Saviour, who supplied an all-sufficient solution to fulfill Heaven's demands and furnish humanity's needs. His intrinsic merit, His majestic power, and His strategic office assure us that "He is able . . . to save them to the uttermost that come unto God by Him" (Heb. 7:25).

THE HERALD OF THE GLAD TIDINGS

How beautiful upon the mountains are the feet of him that bringeth good tidings, that publisheth peace; that bringeth good tidings of good, that publisheth salvation (Is. 52:7).

Christ Himself brought to earth the evangel from the glory; He is the greatest Herald of the Glad Tidings and the most distinguished Publisher of Peace that ever came into the world. He was unshackled from dependence on human decisions and uncircumscribed by earthly demarcations of nation, race, color, or caste. He did not need to stammer or stutter about qualifications; the very nobility of the name He bore was a sufficient commendation, and the nature of His message and ministry supplied the clearest confirmation of His credentials. David's ability as a warrior was best attested by the head of Goliath swinging in His hand; Christ's appointment as a Herald was fully affirmed by the words He spoke and the wonders His words wrought in stilling the storm, supplying the bread, and summoning Lazarus from the grave. "Never man spake like this man."

This Messenger affirmed emphatically, "We speak that We do know and testify that We have seen; and ye receive not Our witness." The fortitude of His fearless faithfulness was fervent and fragrant. He never brought the preciousness of truth into discredit, nor trifled in His testimony to holy things. He rightly represented the One that sent Him and fully revealed the truth committed to Him to communicate. "Only the words that My Father hath given Me do I speak." Therefore His statements and sayings were heaven-hewn and royal. His integrity in respect to the honor of God, His fidelity to the truth entrusted, and His constancy in witnessing for Heaven were without reproach.

Isaiah affirms in chapter 52: "My servant shall deal prudently" (verse 13). He never exaggerated or minimized; He was free from all speculative inferences and sensational incitements; He never needed to retract a single statement or modify the meaning of a word He uttered. He set heavenly verities against human voices.

> Oh, Christ! there is no sweeter theme than Thine,
> That heralds to a restless world God's peace;
> No truth nor tidings ever did enshrine
> So grand a message of such full release.

Christ needed no blare of trumpets or laurel chaplets to amplify the authority of His words. The world has known many wonderful speakers but nothing of their oratory can compare with the dictum of Christ's Gospel.

Plato, the prince of philosophers, had a keen insight into men and things and groped after the truth of immortality. The great Spartan, Solon, the lawgiver of Athens, with his contempt for pomp and pageantry, so impressed his code upon the people that it lasted five hundred years. Roman Cicero, the giant of the Forum, was so fluent and persuasive with his words that he made a stern Caesar tremble and turn pale. If we turn to ethnic leaders of religion, Buddha, six centuries B. C., introduced his system of nirvana, which is self-mortification. Confucius, about 551 to 479 B. C., with his wise code of relationships and obedience, submitted his teaching concerning parent to child, master to servant, subject and state. Mohammed instigated the Koran, which has attracted millions with its ritual and practice.

But the fact ever remains: "Never man spake like this man." Towering loftily above all other leaders, even as far as the heavens are above the earth, stands this Herald of all heralds, Jesus of Nazareth. What is it that differentiates Him so widely from all the rest? Why such superior capacities and such sublime capabilities? How may we account for His awareness of everything and everybody everywhere? Whence His unique oratory and unusual originality?

As to His oratory, He Himself exemplified all that He taught. He Himself exhibited that He was the center and substance of His message. He Himself expressed the glory of God and the truth of His message, and in His own person constituted the foundation of the kingdom of God.

As to His originality, His sublime plan of endeavor was not local, parochial, or national, but world-wide in its appeal and aim. His subject matter was not secondhand or borrowed. He was the voice, not the echo, and the voice could be seen (Rev. 1:12). In His sublime ministry, by the selecting of lilies, sparrows, seed, and trees, He ennobled things most common. His sovereign authority wielded a vocabulary that wrought wonders in the physical, social, and spiritual realms. His supernatural voice awoke the dead, and He declared that His word would one day awaken all that are in the graves and arraign them before His tribunal. His sympathetic love left a trail of healing and a tide of joy wherever He went throughout the land. His sufficient resource was adequate enough to supply all needed help to every class and character that approached Him for aid.

Christ spoke authentically the words of God (John 7:16). He spoke authoritatively with power (Matt. 7:29). He spoke assuredly the truth (John 14:6). He spoke assuringly of peace (John 20:19-20). He spoke appealingly of life (John 6:63). He spoke arrestingly of the unseen (John 14:1; 17:5). He spoke availingly for health and strength (John 4:5).

As Heaven's Herald He understands the divine language and is able to speak to God on man's behalf; He understands human language and is able to speak to man on God's behalf. He is also able to convey a message to the heart as well as the ear. No previous messenger had the ability to do what He did (Luke 24:27). The repleteness of His knowledge, the range of His experience, and the resource of His power made Him the greatest Herald that ever witnessed of heavenly things to humanity. No boast of heraldry was His, nor pomp of power, but love for men.

> Beyond earth's golden glitter lies Heaven's glory,
> From whence He came with love's immortal story.

I

The mysterious name by which God identified Himself at Mount Horeb is later confirmed by Christ in a manifest intimacy in the Gospel. The book of the Revelation completes the interpretation by fully identifying Christ in His majestic infinity as the great I Am.

The I AM OF IMMUTABILITY (Ex. 3:4-6)
    The greatest guarantee ever given.
The I AM OF IDENTITY (Ex. 3:14)
    The Creator identifies Himself by name.
The I AM OF INTEGRITY (Ex. 6:2-5)
    The constancy of the Covenant-maker.
The I AM OF INDEFATIGABILITY (Ex. 6:6-8)
    A verbal and volitional verification.
The I AM OF INVARIABILITY (Ex. 15:11)
    The generous and gracious Guardian.
The I AM OF IMPARTIALITY (Ex. 20:1-3)
    He liberates before He legislates.
The I AM OF INTREPIDITY (Ex. 31:13)
    His purpose is to sanctify and satisfy.
The I AM OF INTERMINABILITY (John 6:35)
    The name of strength and sufficiency.
The I AM OF INDISPENSABILITY (John 8:12)
    The name of splendor and sublimity.
The I AM OF INTIMACY (John 10:7)
    The name of salvation and security.
The I AM OF INDIVIDUALITY (John 10:11)
    The name of sacrifice and sympathy.

The I AM OF INDESTRUCTIBILITY (John 11:25)
 The name of survival and sovereignty.
The I AM OF INSUPERABILITY (John 14:6)
 The name of stateliness and suitability.
The I AM OF INSEPARABILITY (John 15:1)
 The name of supply and superiority.
The I AM OF INIMITABILITY (Rev. 1:8)
 The Wellspring of the wealth of wisdom.
The I AM OF INEXHAUSTIBILITY (Rev. 1:11)
 The true Source of the treasures of truth.
The I AM OF INVINCIBILITY (Rev. 1:7)
 The Founder of the fullness of faith.
The I AM OF IMMORTALITY (Rev. 1:18)
 The Base of all benefits and blessings.
The I AM OF ILLIMITABILITY (Rev. 21:5-6)
 The Maker, Molder, and Master of all things.
The I AM OF INFINITY (Rev. 22:13)
 The Originator of order and objective.
The I AM OF INCOMPREHENSIBILITY (Rev. 22:16)
 The Fountain of fidelity and felicity.

I AM THAT I AM . . .
this is My name forever (Ex. 3:14-15)

To His name there is no norm
To His fame there is no finality
To His claim there is no confine
To His love there is no limit
To His honor there is no horizon
To His beauty there is no boundary
To His truth there is no terminus
To His mercy there is no measure

I AM Jesus (Act 9:5)

A fame that spans the ages,
 A name that soars on high,

The greatest of the sages,
   The Saviour ever nigh.

The brightest of the holy,
   Yet gentlest in His might,
The meekest of the lowly,
   The Lord of love and light.

The sweetest of the precious,
   The fairest of the strong,
The kindest of the gracious,
   The Theme of heavenly song.

The angel of Jehovah,
   The perfect One and just,
Who builds a home forever,
   Where raging storms are hushed.

The bravest of the noble,
   Most generous in His love,
Whose name and fame are global,
   On earth, in Heaven above.

The greatest of the glorious,
   The grandest of the true,
The purest of the righteous,
   Who maketh all things new.

The choicest of the stately,
   The loftiest of the free,
The highest of the heavenly,
   Who reigns eternally.

                    C. J. R.

I am Alpha and Omega (Rev. 22:13)

The self-revelation of the eternal One is given in the Name
which is highest and holiest, *Ehyeh Asher Ehyeh,* **I Am that I**

Am, I will be that I will be. This mysterious utterance is the self-expression of the Eternal, who was later to make Himself manifest in the midst of mankind through the medium of Messiah the Prince, whose many-sided ministry and manifold majesty demonstrate that He is the one Mediator between God and men. The accumulated excellencies and amalgamated energies enshrined in Christ declare Him to be "the image of the invisible God" (Col. 1:15). The inimitable likeness and ineffable loveliness of glory and beauty reflected by Christ entitled Him to affirm, "He that hath seen Me hath seen the Father" (John 14:9). His stately superiority which was disclosed in sovereign sufficiency and sublime sympathy, through the expressions of His will, wisdom, and work, accounted for His saying most assuredly, "I and My Father are one" (John 10:30). By virtue of His exercising almighty power and His expounding the authoritative purpose of God, He emphasizes the fact that the Father hath given all things into His hands (John 13:3). The evidential token of His mastery over death demonstrated at the grave of Lazarus leads Him to expatiate on a coming hour when all that are in the graves will hear His voice and come forth (John 5:25).

The Name, *I AM THAT I AM,* conveys to us a glimpse of the infinities centered in Deity. The Name suggests I am the continual One continually, I am the constant One constantly, I am the perfect One perpetually, I am the steadfast One steadfastly, I am the presiding One permanently, I am the essential One eternally, I am the excellent One everlastingly. From His eternal and divine reality of infinite being, the Lord God defines His solitary dignity, and expresses His enduring personality through the medium of speech, by declaring who and what He is intrinsically, inherently, and immutably. So that the One who is ever vigorous, virtuous, and victorious expresses His Name to the creatures He has created, and then proceeds to explain something of what that Name involves and implies in relation to meeting human needs and satisfying the human heart. *I AM THAT I AM* is a miracle of language.

This Name is unfolded in later revelation as the citadel of omnipotent might, omniscient mind, and omnipresent mercy.

Yea, hereby we approach and enter the castle of infinities, including incorruptibility, immortality, inexhaustibility, indestructibility, impregnability, infallibility, immutability, and such like, and in every case these characteristics apply to His being, wisdom, power, holiness, justice, goodness, and truth, together with all other attributes of His deity. From the very essence of originating entity, all other titles and names of Godhead emerge, all virtuous attributes arise, and all the magnificent perfections in their multiplicity pour forth their celestial radiance and renown. His Name is the effulgent fullness of all the brightest glories of light, the essential essence of the deepest mysteries of life, and the exuberant ecstasies of the highest secrets of love. His Name baffles exposition, His titles are altogether beyond calculation, and the wealth of His designations bewilders every means of valuation.

The Lord revealed to man the grandeur of His glorious character gradually and progressively, the realization of the fullness of the Name depending upon the recognition of the fullness of the time of human need. *I AM THAT I AM* is unintelligible to the natural understanding. "Eye hath not seen, nor ear heard, neither have entered into the heart of man, the things which God hath prepared for them that love Him" (1 Cor. 2:9), was declared to the pundits of human philosophy at the very zenith of their reasoning attainments. Human reason is lost in traversing this tideless ocean of God's unfathomable wisdom. The self-expression of Deity to humanity stands in broader contrast than if the sun deigned in the voluminous magnitude of its magnificent splendor to tell a tiny violet some of the profoundest secrets of light.

Three complete presentations are given in the Scriptures in order to set forth the prerogatives and potentialities incorporated in this wonderful Name. We may speak of these as the seven assurances to arrest admiration and aspiration toward the omnipotent One; secondly, the seven advantages to attract attention and affection to the omnipresent One; and thirdly, the seven attributes to attest the able administration and adjust adoration by the directing of all praise and worship to the omniscient One who alone is worthy (Rev. 5:12).

We shall now proceed to survey seven statements of supremacy declaring ability, seven symbols of sufficiency demonstrating affinity, and seven secrets of superiority displaying authority as attached to the divine designation, *I AM*.

THE I AM OF IMMUTABILITY

> Moses, Moses. And he said, Here am I. And He said, Draw not hither: put off thy shoes from off thy feet; for the place whereon thou standest is holy ground. Moreover He said, I am the God of thy father, the God of Abraham, the God of Isaac, and the God of Jacob (Ex. 3:4-6).
>
> But as touching the resurrection of the dead, have ye not read that which was spoken to you by God, saying, I am the God of Abraham, and the God of Isaac, and the God of Jacob? God is not the God of the dead, but of the living (Matt. 22:31-32).

The Almighty that appeared to Abraham four centuries before and pledged to protect him as a Shield and preserve him as a Sustainer, is none other than the illimitable I Am. The vision and voice that Abraham saw and heard on Mount Moriah is from the same source as that which Moses encountered on Mount Horeb. Both these mountains are called "the mount of God." It was on the first that the patriarch heard his name repeated, Abraham, Abraham; while on the second the lawgiver heard his name repeated, Moses, Moses. Stephen, the martyr, in his fearless faith, was directed by the Spirit of God to quote the above portion, "I am the God of thy fathers, the God of Abraham, and the God of Isaac, and the God of Jacob." In his doing so, Saul of Tarsus, who stood by, heard it (Acts 7:30-34). Not long after Stephen's death, Saul the persecutor saw a vision and heard a voice saying, "Saul, Saul, why persecutest thou Me? And he said, Who art Thou, Lord? And the Lord said, I am Jesus" (Acts 9:4-5). The one who spoke on Moriah saying, "Abraham, Abraham," and on Horeb saying, "Moses, Moses," is the same who said in the Hebrew tongue on the hills of Damascus, "Saul, Saul." The four instances in the Old Testament where the double name is used when addressing individuals are spoken by the One who declares, "I am Jehovah"; while the three occasions in the New Testament are spoken by the One who declares, "I am Jesus" (Acts 9:5). These are one and the same person speaking.

Nothing of importance has been written on this specific subject, although the Name is the divine imprimatur of confirmation, which vouches for the historicity, authority, veracity, authenticity, and infallibility of Scripture. The eternal God has put His signature to revealed truth. This sovereign declaration, "I am the God of Abraham, the God of Isaac, and the God of Jacob," confirms the entire history of the patriarchs in the book of Genesis. The three patriarchal names are used together on forty-two occasions in the Old Testament Scriptures, in relation to the promise, the oath, and the covenant, a veritable hallmark of inspiration.

The divine Name furnishes a firm foundation in support of the sacred covenants, an opalescent ornament of distinction to the ordained oracles, and a trustworthy tribute to the theme of the Testaments. This Name is above every name: "I am Jesus."

So then, the venture of the faith of Abraham in his departure from his own country was of divine promotion, the veneration of the faith of Isaac, who was famous for his Godly fear, was God-produced, and the vitality of the faith Jacob expressed in his twelve sons is also attributable to the authority and authorship of the ageless I AM. These statements are fully ratified and confirmed in the Epistle to the Hebrews, where Christ is presented not only as Creator but as the Author and Finisher, Captain and Completer, Promoter and Perfector, Fountain and Fullness, Commencer and Consummator, yea the Founder and Finalizer of all aspects of the life of faith. Well did Isaiah say, "Hearken unto Me, O Jacob and Israel, My called; I am He; I am the first, I also am the last. Mine hand also hath laid the foundation of the earth, and My right hand hath spanned the heavens" (Is. 48:12-13).

The faith of Abraham was characterized by an exclusive simplicity and exceptional splendor, from the time he built his first altar on the rock Moreh at the top of Mount Gerazim, until he erected the seventh and last on the rock Moriah at

Jerusalem. He had a clear comprehension of the character of God and trusted implicitly. He believed the two immutables of promise and oath which God gave to him, and when he had patiently endured he inherited the promise (Heb. 6:15).

If we have any misconceptions as to whether Christ preceded Abraham, let us listen while He tells us plainly: "Abraham rejoiced to see My day: and he saw it, and was glad. Then said the Jews unto Him, Thou art not yet fifty years old, and hast thou seen Abraham? Jesus said unto them, Verily, verily, I say unto you, Before Abraham was, I am" (John 8:56-58).

How gratifying it is to know there is One to whom an eternal purpose has been entrusted for fulfillment, who is absolutely trustworthy. Our Lord is characterized by an extraordinary determination and exquisite devotion, and these are combined with a most friendly kindness and kingly faithfulness which make Him especially lovable and laudable (Heb. 1:9).

> Summer and winter, springtime and harvest,
> Sun, moon, and stars in their courses above,
> Join with all nature in manifold witness,
> To Thy great faithfulness, mercy, and love.
>
> Great is Thy faithfulness! Great is Thy faithfulness!
> Morning by morning new mercies I see;
> All I have needed Thy hand hath provided,
> Great is Thy faithfulness, Lord, unto me!

T. O. CHISHOLM

THE I AM OF IDENTITY

> And God said unto Moses, I AM THAT I AM: and He said, Thus shalt thou say unto the children of Israel, I AM hath sent me unto you. . . This is My name for ever, and this is My memorial unto all generations (Ex. 3:14-15).

No name ever breathed is so pregnant in mystery and persistent in majesty as this one, expressing as it does the personal entity of Deity. Eternal being is the essential source and the essence of all vitality, volition, and vision. Here we meet with sublimity in simplicity, the maximum in minimum, the undefinable defined in a spoken definition, the inexplicable is expressed in the words *I AM THAT I AM.*

The occasion of this revelation is of deep interest. God had previously expressed His title *Elohim* to the patriarchs, which by its meaning suggests the God who wills all that He does. He now tells Moses that He is about to make Himself known to Israel as Jehovah, by demonstrating Himself as the God who does all that He wills. The *Ehyeh Asher Ehyeh* is the name of the eternal entity and essential energy in personality, a designation which stands behind all other names and titles of Godhead. *I AM* expresses the completeness of intellectual, volitional, and emotional capacities, in their perfect equipoise and absolute harmony of holiness.

Such a mind, will, and heart are shown to be displeased and disturbed by the oppression and persecution imposed by the Egyptian world power on a covenanted people. The One who expressed Himself at a flaming desert bush burning and unconsumed, supplied an instructive illustration to Moses of the timeless, changeless, tireless character of the divine nature. Therefore, when the scepter of such dominion determines a deliverance for an enslaved people, no terrestrial or infernal power can prevent it.

Incorporated in the breadth and beauty of this blessed Name is everything of omnipotence, omniscience, and omnipresence, and also the totality of prescience, providence, and permanence, all of which we shall find verified in the "I am's" of Christ in the Gospel of John. We should observe that the Lord uses the first personal pronoun, *I*, eighteen times in the profound declarations of the chapter we are considering; while a threefold reference is made to the renowned patriarchs, Abraham, Isaac, and Jacob. Let us also pause and consider that through the never-to-be-forgotten notoriety of this Name we are assured of the accuracy and authority of the Scriptures of truth in their authenticity, veracity, and inerrancy.

This Name is like a piece of massive masonry that forms the foundation stone of all revelation, that furnishes the chief cornerstone of covenant confirmation, and forever fashions the coping stone that crowns with completeness the spiritual blessings of salvation. We may bring every factor of research to bear upon the unprecedented treasures stored in His everlasting Name, and examine its potentials with a microscope from every phase which is, which was, and which is to come, scrutinize its proportions with the telescope from everlasting to everlasting, and concentrate on its perfections of Urim and Thummim with the spectroscope, to bring into visibility the many variegated glories that pertain to it, and we shall arrive at one verdict: His Name is above every name, whether it be in regard to life, love, or light. Remember His is the everlasting life (John 3:16), the everlasting love (Jer. 31:3), and the everlasting light (Is. 60:19-20).

Infinite importance clusters about the incidentals of this unveiling. The most miraculous and marvelous of wondrous experiences was granted to Moses on this occasion when the all-glorious Lord, who is arrayed in gorgeous light, deigned in His gracious love to do the most generous thing, namely, that of introducing and expressing Himself by revealing His very identity, to one who was destined to become the first national emancipator. The experience greatly ennobled the character of Moses, enlarged his capacities, enriched his conceptions, and enabled him to endure as seeing Him who is invisible (Heb. 11:27). Centuries later Moses was one of the chosen to stand with Christ on the mount of transfiguration and speak with Him of His decease which He was about to accomplish at Jerusalem for the emancipation of mankind, from the thraldom of sin (Luke 9:30).

In the present case, the inexpressively illustrious Lord, who is Himself the Inaugurator of life, the Irradiator of light, and the Interpreter of love, is about to make known His character as the Instigator of national liberty, and Emancipator of the enslaved. Therefore, in order to affirm the project, to announce the purpose and assure the power for its fulfillment, He reveals His peerless Name, *I AM THAT I AM.* Herein is incorporated the whole casket of the Lord's credentials, the complete catalog of His capabilities and also the impregnable castle of His faithful constancy.

When we take into account the fabulous wealth associated with conspicuous names in history, the famous wisdom attached to the names of outstanding philosophers, the enormous works achieved by pioneering engineers, builders, and contractors, the prodigious writings of clever men of genius, the marvelous wonders discovered by physicists and giants of scientific lore and all the worthy names of rulers, judges, and physicians, what an enormous list there is available. Yet withal, excelling and exceeding the combined honors of all these, standing first in order of precedency, best in ranks of excellency, most in degree of superiority, and last in state of finality is the Name above every name, the Name of our Lord and Saviour Jesus Christ. The one choicest in character bears this lordly Name; He is highest in fame and justly wears it; He is noblest in nature and fitly airs it; "there is none like Him."

How much we need to repair again and again to that state in which Moses stood, and seek a fresh glimpse of the greatness and glory of His Name. We have known times when the mind becomes temporarily detached from the transient things of life and the towering mountaintops are left far beneath; when the claims of earth seemed momentarily severed, its charms of beauty broken, and its cares and conflicts silenced. Then the soul soars to heights of transcendent calm that slowly merge into the majestic harmonies of heavenly music, where, amid the radiant light of mystic glory, in cloudless day, we visualize angels ceaselessly serving the One in the midst of the throne of the Heaven of heavens, who bears the Name that is above every name, "the blessed and only Potentate, the King of kings and Lord of lords" (1 Tim. 6:15). This is the vision glorious of which Paul speaks (2 Cor. 12:3).

> Jesus is the sweetest name I know,
> And He's just the same as His lovely name,
> And that's the reason why I love Him so;
> Oh, Jesus is the sweetest name I know.

> LELA LONG

THE I AM OF INTEGRITY

And God spake unto Moses, and said unto him, I am Jehovah: and I appeared unto Abraham, unto Isaac, and unto Jacob, by the name of God Almighty, but by My name Jehovah was I not known to them. And I have also established My covenant . . . and I have remembered My covenant (Ex. 6:2-5 ASV).

The thrice repeated "I have" in verses 4 and 5 of Exodus 6 supplies the verification that the pledges made to the patriarchs were being honored. The divine integrity is morally sound, marshally strong, and mightily sure. When the Lord said to Abraham, "I will bless thee . . . and thou shalt be a blessing" (Gen. 12:2), He meant what He said, and at the close of his earthly career the confirmation of the promise is recorded, "The LORD had blessed Abraham in all things" (Gen. 24:1).

Covenant faithfulness is one of the highlights in the lovingkindness of the divine character and is both intensive in its reality and extensive in its range, for David speaks of it as reaching to the skies (Ps. 36:5 margin). God's reputation for constancy and integrity constitutes an immovable rock foundation on which we may rely confidently and rest contentedly. We do well to remember God's faithfulness is immortally linked most intricately and exquisitely with His justice, purity, truth, and love, in an all-holy unison. From the very dawn of the declaration of His being a faithful God (Deut. 7:9), to the high noon of its display in the book of the Revelation, there is not a trace of variableness or shadow of turning. The imperishable garland of fadeless glory rests on the head of impregnable faithfulness, and the luster of its burnish, the sheen of its untarnished beauty, and the scope of its unstinted bounty abide the ages.

Joshua rehearsed God's fidelity to His promise before the entire nation. "Behold, this day I am going the way of all the earth: and ye know in all your hearts and in all your souls, that not one thing hath failed of all the good things which the LORD your God spake concerning you; all are come to pass unto you, and not one thing hath failed thereof" (Josh. 23:14). David recorded it, for among his last words he said, "Yet He hath made with me an everlasting covenant, ordered in all things, and sure: for this is all my salvation, and all my desire" (2 Sam. 23:5). Ethan remembered it in a covenant psalm in which he uses faithfulness seven times: "I will sing of the lovingkindness of Jehovah for ever: With my mouth will I make known Thy faithfulness to all generations. For I have said, Mercy shall be built up for ever; Thy faithfulness wilt Thou establish in the very heavens" (Ps. 89:1-2 RV). Isaiah re-echoes it relative to Messiah, "Righteousness shall be the girdle of His loins, and faithfulness the girdle of His reins" (Is. 11:5). Hosea registers it: "Yea, I will betroth thee unto Me in righteousness, and in judgment, and in lovingkindness, and in mercies. I will even betroth thee unto Me in faithfulness" (Hos. 2:19-20). Paul re-emphasized it: "It is a faithful saying: For if we be dead with Him, we shall also live with Him: if we suffer, we shall also reign with Him: if we deny Him, He also will deny us: If we believe not, yet He abideth faithful: He cannot deny Himself" (2 Tim. 2:11-13). In the midst of grim calamity, Jeremiah recalled the same and said, "Therefore have I hope. It is of the LORD's mercies that we are not consumed, because His compassions fail not. They are new every morning: great is Thy faithfulness. The LORD is my portion, saith my soul; therefore will I hope in Him" (Lam. 3:21-24).

The five occurrences of the word "hope" in the immediate context indicate that the Lord's faithfulness is one of the most potent incentives, inspiring our expectation and instilling new energy into our effort. Be assured, the unshakable foundations of our covenanted salvation are wholly imperishable, because of the unalterable and unchangeable faithfulness of the Lord our God. His precious promises can never be imperiled, for the Saviour will not and must not allow anyone to endanger His reputation for constancy, integrity, and fidelity. The truth of His Word is guaranteed forever by His indescribable Name, which is indelibly written by His eternal Spirit. Wherefore, consider Him, concentrate upon His character that is so clearly intimated in His self-revelation, I AM THAT I AM, steadfast in faithfulness, resolute in righteousness, absolute in justice, and in loving-kindness. "I AM"; "I will"; "I have."

THE I AM OF INDEFATIGABILITY

Wherefore say unto the children of Israel, I am Jehovah, and I will bring you out from under the burdens of the Egyptians . . . I will redeem you with an outstretched arm, and with great judgments . . . I will take you to Me for a people, and I will be to you a God; and ye shall know that I am Jehovah your God. . . . And I will bring you in unto the land which I sware to give to Abraham, to Isaac, and to Jacob; and I will give it you for a heritage: I am Jehovah (Ex. 6:6-8 ASV).

An indefatigable nature knows nothing of fatigue or faintness and this is the very character of God conveyed centuries later to the nation of Israel by the prophet when he asked, "Hast thou not known? hast thou not heard? The everlasting God, Jehovah, the Creator of the ends of the earth, fainteth not, neither is weary" (Is. 40:28 ASV). Because He is so great in might and so strong in power, no star among the myriads that are in the heavens ever fails. He it is who measured the waters accurately with two parts of hydrogen to one of oxygen. He also meted out heaven consistently and orderly so that eclipses, equinoxes, seedtime and harvest, summer and winter, day and night are unvariable in their regularity. He has clearly in mind the cubical content of the dust of the earth, and the mountains and hills He has weighed in a balance so that every element therein is compounded proportionately by a mathematical formula of tabulation, as every reputable physicist knows well (Is. 40:12). The four facts about God's hand as an indication of His might and majesty should be carefully considered.

The understanding of the great I AM is unsearchable and His mind inscrutable. Combined with these attributes He Himself is indefatigable, for He never faints, yea, nor can He fail or be discouraged in His magnificent purpose (Is. 42:4). Emanating from His unwearying disposition arise His determination and decision, which is so wonderfully expressed in the seven I will's of this portion conjoined as they are with the threefold declaration of the far-famed title, I AM.

Notice the steadfast resolve: I will bring you out; the sovereign rescue: I will rid you of bondage; the stipulated ransom: I will redeem you; the stately relationship: I will take you to Me for a people; the sublime reason: I will be to you a God; the spacious release: I will bring you into the land; and the settled recompense: I will give it you for a heritage.

The Lord emphatically re-affirms what He is and what He intends to do, which is very essential, if the nation in its dilemma is to be reheartened with fresh hope. Likewise, the grave condition of the whole Gentile world, described in the opening chapter of Romans, made necessary, if hope was to be awakened, the declaration of the determined purpose of God, set forth in chapter 8. Therefore hope is referred to more frequently in the message to the church at Rome than in any book in the New Testament and in this light God is called "the God of hope" (Rom. 15:13).

What a blessed assurance it is to know that the One who has the authority and ability to perform all that He announces is Himself the Pioneer of promise, the Proprietor of providence, the Promoter of covenants, and the same who purposed an eternal purpose before the world began unto our glory. In the fulfilling of His pledges and promises His name is glorified and His nature magnified, as the God of faithfulness and truth. He is continually observant of all that transpires because he is omniscient, He is prominent everywhere to assure and aid because He is the omnipresent One, and He is efficient always because He is omnipotent. In the veracity of His Word, we may have a confident trust in His ability and an undivided allegiance to His authority. By virtue of His competent power and covenant pledge, none can prevent Him from carrying through to consummation His eternal purpose.

THE I AM OF INVARIABILITY

Who is like unto Thee, O Jehovah, among the gods? . . .
Jehovah shall reign for ever and ever. . . . If thou wilt diligently
hearken to the voice of Jehovah thy God, and wilt do that which

is right in His eyes, and wilt give ear to His commandments, and keep all His statutes, I will put none of the diseases upon thee, which I have put upon the Egyptians: for I am Jehovah that healeth thee (Ex. 15:11,18,26 ASV).

That glorious Name is here identified with additional splendor by virtue of what the Lord wrought for the nation. The imperial might of His majesty forms a glowing background which colorfully reflects the blended beauties of His impressive mercy. The sovereign Lord, so supreme in His delivering strength, is also the sympathetic Shepherd, who sustains and secures His ransomed flock by providing the requisites required to fully establish the emancipation.

Initial things are usually important and this interesting record is the first occurrence of song in the Bible. Never before had the shore of any sea reverberated with the melodious outburst of a multitude singing a deathless song of praise to the Most High. Centuries later, the prophet Hosea reminded the nation of this notable event (Hos. 2:15). Not only so, but the deliverance is focused through the ages to find its utmost completion, not at the Red Sea, but at the crystal sea, where an innumerable host swells the song of everlasting salvation, in celebration of the final victory over evil and the full emancipation from a defeated and depleted foe (Rev. 15:2-4). The Spirit of God is responsible for the words written by Moses, for they are incorporated as the song of the Lamb, to herald that more famous triumph which He gained for mankind.

Truly the offering of the Passover lamb was a real factor in their deliverance from a physical enemy in Egypt, where they were held in cruel bondage, but they needed a greater deliverance from the power of evil itself, that was enslaving the soul. The people had been brought out from the distress of Egypt but they met a new dilemma at Marah. The nature of sin is likened in Scripture to a loathsome disease, and therefore after the tragedy and calamity of their slavery had been overcome, the inner soul-malady manifests itself, showing that they were yet in the gall of bitterness and bond of iniquity. At Marah they murmured against Moses, who cried mightily unto the Lord. The divine prescience or foreknowledge of the Lord

Himself, which is so apparent in these events, is linked with His providence. Years before this crisis He had prepared a tree which He now ordered Moses to cut down and cast into the bitter waters, and the waters were made sweet. We need the added assurance after our emancipation which Paul affirms: "Sin shall not have dominion over you" (Rom. 6:14).

The One who is stationed highest in heavenly honor, described as being glorious in holiness and fearful in praises (verse 10), in sacred mystery became manifest in human form. As the incarnate deity, He was cut off as a vicarious sacrifice, dying as the Just for the unjust that He might bring us to God. The penalty of our perversity was borne by Him and "with His stripes we are healed" (Is. 53:5). Wherefore, when demonstrating these verities at Marah the Saviour says, "I am Jehovah that healeth thee."

The bitterest agony of our Saviour's unfathomable grief is expressed in His heart-rending cry, "My God, My God, why hast Thou forsaken Me?" Lo, "He was made sin for us"; wherefore, in His dire distress of soul, featured in another plea, He utters these words: "I said, O my God, take me not away in the midst of my days" (Ps. 102:24). Christ grappled with the grim giant of human grief and gained a glorious victory. He surmounted the surging waves of human sorrow and struck a deathblow at their cause. He broke the brazen bars of the dungeon of darkness and brought back the benighted captives to light and liberty. He turned the tide of human trials by making them a means of testing and tempering to promote a richer testimony. He alters the trend of the tornado of terror and transforms the valley of Achor with its tears and tombs to a triumphal gate of entry so that we may have access into the warmth and welcome of a fadeless inheritance.

"Blessed be the Name, blessed be the Name of the Lord," for the radiant light of His high honor and the redolent love of His holy heart shine brightest and seem kindest when He Himself appears robed in the garments of sacrifice. The glorious I AM becomes our gracious healer, and who is sufficient to make known the matchless worthiness of such a Saviour? No wonder we find our finest words too feeble to express the fullness of His grace and love. Our richest rhetoric is far too restricted in range to recount the repleteness of His resources which are held in reserve. Even the choicest comparisons we endeavor to make are far too circumscribed to commend adequately the comeliness of His lovely countenance. When Jeremiah realized in measure these realities he said, "There is none like unto Thee, O Jehovah; Thou art great, and Thy name is great in might. Who should not fear Thee, O King of the nations? for to Thee doth it appertain; forasmuch as among all the wise men of the nations, and in all their royal estate, there is none like unto Thee. But Jehovah is the true God; He is the living God, and an everlasting King" (Jer. 10:6-7,10 ASV).

THE I AM OF IMPARTIALITY

> And God spake all these words, saying, I am Jehovah thy God, who brought thee out of the land of Egypt, out of the house of bondage. Thou shalt have no other gods before Me (Ex. 20:1-3; Deut. 5:6 ASV).

The Lord first demonstrates His matchless power as a Deliverer from cruel bondage before He makes request for the devotion of His people. He bases what He requires of them on what He does for them; He first redeems and liberates before he enjoins them to love and obey Him. Therefore that which John states in the New Testament is forever true: "We love Him, because He first loved us." This is love's logic.

The compassion of God emanates from His exquisite character of enduring constancy. His very name voices the virtuous nobility of His unvariable nature. His divine credentials worthily commend Him, while His dignified capabilities wonderfully confirm His competence to complete the counsels of His own immutable will. The formidable undertaking of freeing an enslaved people from ruthless tyranny and emancipating them to true freedom, also entailed the necessity for a plan of immediate maintenance, together with a guarantee that all emergencies would be fully met. What better means of assurance could possibly have been given than that of rehearsing the incomparable Name, "I am Jehovah thy God." The wonderful deliverances which had already been wrought were a telling demonstration of the absolute dominion wielded by the Lord Himself. By virtue of His perfect leadership, He brought them out of the land of Egypt and liberated them as a people. Then in His prevailing lordship He legislated for their welfare and stressed the necessity of their revering His Name: "Thou shalt not take the name of the Lord thy God in vain" (Ex. 20:7).

The Name of Deity indicates the divine nature, and the very fact that God sought their love was an index to His own faultless character, which is expressed in the words used centuries later by the Apostle John: "God is love." During the manifestation, Christ verified this great truth, for He reduced the 613 precepts of the law into two specific commands, by saying, "Thou shalt love the Lord thy God with all thy heart, and with all thy soul, and with all thy mind. This is the first and great commandment. And the second is like unto it, Thou shalt love thy neighbor as thyself. On these two commandments hang all the law and the prophets" (Matt. 22:37-40). Wherefore we are not surprised to hear Paul the apostle say, "For all the law is fulfilled in one word, even in this; Thou shalt love thy neighbor as thyself" (Gal. 5:14). This is not human love but the fruit of Romans 5:5.

When our Lord is appropriating this divine title and applying it to Himself, He confirms that He is the embodiment of all virtuous grace and vigorous goodness, for He displays in the exercise of His ministry victorious government for human well-being in every sphere. He solicits love, too (John 14:15,23; 15:9-10; 21:15-17), yea, and enjoins it toward others (John 15:12,17). Christ declared this to be one of the supreme evidences of Christianity (John 13:35), and it certainly constitutes the very eye of discernment and heart of devotion (1 John 3:16).

The summit of love's perfection is revealed in Christ, whose perfect love John assures us perfects our love and casts out fear (1 John 4:17-18). The means of our being perfected depends on our reaching the full vision of perfectness: "When we see

Him we shall be like Him."

The light of the glory of God's ineffable love and immortal loveliness is revealed in the face of Jesus Christ. The very essence of the effulgence and the excellence of endurance that characterize love, have their source and abode in Godhead. Wherefore the mind of love, the will of love, and the heart of love are all centered in Christ Jesus. In spite of the multiplied restrictions and manifold hindrances of our environment, the pathway to the largest of liberties is unbarred. A responsive obedience opens the gate to the mount of vision, enabling each saint to gaze as with unveiled face on the glory of the Lord, and to be changed into the same image (2 Cor. 3:18). His glory is radiant in love's perfect beauty, paramount in immaculate purity, and vibrant with the music of abiding harmony amid supernal splendor.

Love surmounts all obstacles and can never be superseded or silenced. Her lustrous scepter and supreme sovereignty last forever, because the strong hand that holds and sways unceasingly never tires. Christ then is our Emancipator and our Liberator from worldly lusts, He delivers and sustains until we are presented faultless before the presence of His glory. Only the ceaseless, the changeless, and continuous I AM exercises the ability, authority, and abidingness to achieve this. The Lord Jehovah reveals Himself to Israel as the loftiest of all legislators, the divinest of all deliverers, the highest of all hierarchies, the ablest of all administrators, the chiefest of all celebrities, and the most excellent of all excellencies.

THE I AM OF INTREPIDITY

> Speak thou also unto the children of Israel, saying, Verily ye shall keep My sabbaths: for it is a sign between Me and you throughout your generations; that ye may know that I am Jehovah who sanctifieth you (Ex. 31:13 ASV).

Here we meet with another great compound title, *I Am Jehovah Mekadeshkem,* which means, "Jehovah your sanctifier." How wondrously resolute the Lord must be when He undertakes to sanctify a multitude of people with all their variableness, make them to be partakers of a similar nature to His own, and adopt them as a holy society into the very household of God. Such a task requires a nameless degree of supernatural wisdom and ability. The One who declares His purpose with such a clear ring of certainty, first of all discloses His identity by stating, "I am Jehovah who sanctifieth you," and this He does in the calm confidence of His inherent capability and constancy and in the clear conception of His inevitable conquest, when He shall consummate His gracious work in absolute holiness.

Let us notice that in the context He bestows the talent on Bezaleel to beautify the sanctuary of God in the tabernacle, which was a very great honor. The tabernacle of the testimony with its types and symbols was the medium through which the Lord testified to Israel the spiritual standards of truth. We should take into account the sevenfold use of the personal pronoun *I* in the first eleven verses of the chapter. This use leads up to the I AM of verse 13. "I have called," "I have filled," and "I have given" express the method of divine appointment for the fashioning and furnishing of the dwelling place.

To distinguish Israel from the surrounding nations, the Lord enjoined His people to participate with Himself in the keeping of a system of seven sabbaths, which included the seventh day, the seventh week, the seventh month, the seventh year, the seven times seven years for the jubilee, and so forth. These are twice stated as being instituted for a sign (verses 13,17). What then did they signify? Obviously God's rest is not entered or secured by the keeping of special days, but these directed the expectation to look for a Person who would establish perfect rest. If we pause for a moment to consider the seventh day, the test of this sabbath was first made with the nation in connection with the manna; in this chapter the test is in relation to the tabernacle. Both the manna and the tabernacle are figures of Christ. Under law, the slightest disregard or violation of sabbath regulations was visited with swift retribution; but it is a far more heinous sin to disregard and dishonor Christ, who is the true rest. During the manifestation, the Jews maintained they were honoring the sabbath law; Christ disallowed their claim and charged them with dishonoring Him (see John 7:19,23 and 8:49).

We do not now remember a day; we remember a Deliverer. Let us recall it was the Creator who enjoined the keeping of the seventh day, and John is careful to remind us that the Creator was manifested (John 1:3,10). He amended the old order in the New Covenant and endorsed the first day of the week (John 20:1,19), the day commemorating His victorious resurrection. Wherefore, He the Creator does not say in the New Covenant: "Remember the sabbath day, to keep it holy," but as Creator and Redeemer He does say: "This do in remembrance of Me" (Luke 22:19). He takes away the first that He might establish the second.

The teaching of the New Testament is clear both on the fulfillment of the sign of the sabbath, and the ground of our sanctification. Wherefore by His "will we are sanctified through the offering of the body of Jesus Christ once for all . . . . For by one offering He hath perfected for ever them that are sanctified" (Heb. 10:10,14).

He who is inestimably precious and exquisitely glorious has determined to bedeck and beautify His redeemed people and fashion them in the likeness of His own lovely character. We were told earlier of the sanctifying of the tabernacle by His glory, and also of the high priest and his sons (Ex. 29:43-44). Remember it was our great High Priest who prayed, "Sanctify them through Thy truth: Thy word is truth. . . . For their sakes I sanctify Myself, that they also might be sanctified through the truth" (John 17:17,19).

Sanctify was the first word spoken to Israel after they were delivered from Egypt (Ex. 13:1). Over a score of references follow in the remainder of the book. If we combine these with *holy* and *holiness*, together they appear one hundred times. We are familiar with the refrain, "Be ye holy, for I am holy." Today the saints are being beautified by the same Spirit and are being built together for a habitation of God (Eph. 2:22).

How reassuring it is to know that the great I AM in the full strength of His majestic might will persevere with His people, until prevailingly and permanently He accomplishes His will.

If we are to be identified with Deity we must be identical in disposition. Paul the apostle states the matter clearly: "The very God of peace sanctify you wholly; and I pray God your whole spirit and soul and body be preserved blameless unto the coming of our Lord Jesus Christ. Faithful is He that calleth you, who also will do it" (1 Thess. 5:23-24).

What enlightenment! To know that we are endowed, enriched, and exalted by Christ to express the very semblance of His character and wear the perfect likeness of His image. He has assured this by the greatest guarantee ever given and ratified it with a covenant which is sealed with the most authoritative seal ever affixed to a document. This we learn is stamped with the weightiest insignia ever utilized by wealth or wisdom, namely, I AM. Our beloved Lord who has purposed this, is the princeliest of principalities, in rank, in range, and in renown. He is the most noble of all nobilities, the most stately of all sovereignties, the most desirable of all dignitaries, and the most able of all authorities, even God over all, blessed forevermore.

> Join all the glorious names of wisdom, love, and power,
> That mortals ever knew, that angels ever bore;
>   All are too mean to speak His worth,
>   Too mean to set the Saviour forth.

ISAAC WATTS

THE I AM OF INTERMINABILITY

> Jesus said unto them, I am the bread of life: he that cometh to Me shall never hunger; and he that believeth on Me shall never thirst (John 6:35).

The mainspring of the message recorded by John is the creatorship of Christ, which is combined with His progenitorship and judgeship. "All things were made by Him; and without Him was not any thing made that was made" (1:3); therefore the competence of omnipotence is one of the grandest features associated with our Lord's earthly ministry. A divine distinction marks all His declarations and doings, so that His words are wholly warrantable when He affirms that He has the seal of the Father's approval (John 6:27).

Christ made this stupendous claim immediately following the feeding of the multitude and after He had foiled the boisterous storm, in view of an attempt that was being made by some to undervalue such vital evidences of His Messiahship. Wherefore, the national leaders also introduced the matter of Moses and the supply of manna in the wilderness to detract further from the significance of the great sign Christ had wrought. According to their cramped estimate, His meeting the need of a multitude for one single day was wholly unworthy of recognition in the light of the provision Moses made for the whole nation during a forty-year period. Christ answered their reasoning by reminding them that the One who summoned Moses at the burning bush and there demonstrated the changeless character of His resourcefulness, was the real Sustainer of life who had supported them.

When the Lord made reference to the true Bread which came down from Heaven, the people immediately made demands to be given the same, whereupon Christ reponded by saying, "I am the bread of life," a reply which indicates that the age-old symbol of sustenance, manna, was then and there superseded because Christ Himself as the true spiritual Substance had come.

No man had any part in proposing or preparing the manna, no earthly syndicate had the power to procure the right to produce it, and no section of the nation paid for any portion of that which they received during the entire period. Likewise, Christ is not the product of human longing or labor. How could He be, seeing He produced the world? (John 1:10)

Like bread was provided for the physical life of Israel in the wilderness, so Christ, the Bread from Heaven, furnishes every suitable requirement for maintaining the spiritual life of His redeemed people. Nothing pertaining to His character is in any wise detrimental or deficient in the building up of a healthy, hearty, holy Christian life. The comeliness of His qualities, the constituents of His virtues, and the completeness of His perfections comprise the very essence of essential goodness. If we need peace, let us partake of Him, for He is our Peace (Eph. 2:14). If we desire life, let us resort to Him, for He is our Life (Col. 3:4). If we require strength, let us repair to Him, for He is our Strength (Ps. 27:1).

Every element to nourish a vigorous faith, to nurture a virtuous love, and to nerve a vital hope, every requisite to increase righteousness, insure peace, and inspire joy; and every factor to renew the spirit of the mind, replenish the devotion of heart, and restore vivacity to the soul — all these reside in Christ. Notice there are seven special expressions in this discourse, which Christ uses in connection with the I AM title. "Meat which endureth unto everlasting life" (verse 27), "the true bread from heaven" (verse 32), "the bread of God is He which cometh down from heaven" (verse 33), "I am the bread of life" (verse 35), "I am the bread which came down from heaven" (verse 41), "I am the living bread which came down from heaven" (verse 51), "the bread that I will give is My flesh, which I will give for the life of the world" (verse 51). The term, *from Heaven,* is mentioned ten times in the statement to impress upon us the Source of the supply, the suitability of the Bread, and the character of the sustenance contained therein, all of which are alike supernatural.

What a wonderful bestowment this is, Bread from Heaven, brought to mankind by God's beloved Son, He Himself constituting the gift. He is not making reference to His work, wisdom, or will, but to Himself, the very Soul of sustenance, the Substance of salvation, and secret Source of spiritual life. The name of Abraham with its renown retires, the fame of Moses with its grand record recedes, but the name and fame of Christ remain the same.

Have you examined the quality of this Bread from Heaven to ascertain if there is any remarkable difference about it to warrant the claim? Is there anything like it anywhere else in all the world? Has man with his scientific skill been able to reproduce something of similar type? May we obtain an equally suitable substitute to replace it? Has man framed a theory or philosophy of life that makes unnecessary this heavenly source of supply?

To whom shall we go but to Christ, for the precious blood that cleanses, the redeeming grace that delivers, the constant care that maintains, the eternal love that exhilarates, the generous gift that enriches, the mighty power that perfects, and the determined purpose that promotes the final consummation in glory? God has made His Son available, accessible, and adaptable as the living Bread from Heaven, to meet the needs of mankind everywhere and always, for Christ is utterly inexhaustible. This means that a higher life of immortal blessedness is in store for the redeemed of the Lord.

THE I AM OF INDISPENSABILITY

> Then spake Jesus again unto them saying, I am the light of the world: he that followeth Me shall not walk in darkness, but shall have the light of life (John 8:12).

Light is the finest figure of truth and is a word to which Christ made seven references in John 8. Light also stands to represent holiness and spiritual knowledge. Therefore, our Lord's claim to be the Light of the world means much more than the light in the physical universe which emanates from the sun. Christ is the "light of the world" (8:12); "the light of men" (1:4); "the light which lighteth every man that cometh into the world" (1:9); "the light of truth" (Ps. 43:2); "the light of the knowledge of the glory of God" (2 Cor. 4:6); "a light to the Gentiles" (Is. 49:6). All suchlike features of Him are affirmed in the Scriptures.

From the time Sir Isaac Newton discovered the spectrum and found that white light consisted of numerous colorful rays perfectly blended in one, the way was opened for an endless investigation to be made concerning the constituents of light, and what wonderful discoveries have since been made. Our blessed Lord was fully aware of all the rays that would be discovered; He is fully aware of all those that are still unknown to man; and with a perfect consciousness of every feature involved declared emphatically, "I am the light of the world," and assured to all who would follow Him, the light of life. This not only includes an understanding of origins and destiny, but of the greatest knowledge of all, "the knowledge of God," for God is light. No clearer radiance ever shone, as this Gospel proves, to give the true import of the sacrificial lamb (1:29), the sacred temple (2:13-16), the serpent of brass (3:14-16), the Sychar well (4:5-15), the Saviour of the world (4:42), the sheep gate (5:2-9), the sea of Galilee (6:1-27), the sustaining manna (6:31-51), the symbolic feast (7:37-39), the Siloam pool (9:4-7), the Shepherd of Israel (10:1-30), the sepulcher of death (11:35-44), and the secret source of life (15:1). These types were incorporated in Old Testament literature by One who had a perfect knowledge of what they typified.

Christ is the Substance of all shadows, the Subject of all signs and the Sum total of light transparent and radiance translucent. What a clear light He throws upon the path of life by His unfaltering submission, His unfailing service, His unflagging strength, His unfainting supplication, and His unflinching sacrifice.

The brilliance of His radiance has illumined the centuries, introducing the reality of personal Godhead, interpreting the Scriptures of truth, instructing the greatest saints, impelling the noblest service, and inspiring the sweetest songs. What ratification He has given of the veracity of prophecy by virtue of His words and works. With what solemnity He draped the relative sanctity of marriage and the personal responsibility of child care. How vividly the records of national history and regal personalities were flashed upon the screen by the lightrays of His teaching. The reality of eternity has dawned as clear as day by virtue of His disclosure of things to come. The revelation of Deity shone forth in brightest splendor by His unveiling of vital holiness and portrayal of the Father. The radiance of glory reached high noon in presence of the transfiguration of His victorious majesty. The rewards for loyalty in service glistened like costly gems of rare value when He described the divine recompense for devoted labor. The sacredness of marriage assumed new dignity in the light of this beloved Bridegroom.

No one else has extended the range of man's reasoning

powers, nor opened a wider field to his thinking capacity in breadth, length, depth, and height than Christ. What interesting insight He has given into the material things of the universe, what an intimate understanding of physical powers and their potentials He has opened to the mind, what important factors He has imparted to man's knowledge of moral standards, what information He has furnished concerning spiritual virtues and ethical values, and what infinite realities He has unveiled in relation to celestial conditions.

THE I AM OF INTIMACY

> Then said Jesus unto them again, Verily, verily, I say unto you, I am the door of the sheep. All that ever came before Me are thieves and robbers: but the sheep did not hear them. I am the door: by Me if any man enter in, he shall be saved, and shall go in and out, and find pasture (John 10:7-9).

In one of the largest art galleries of Canada hangs a large impressive painting titled, "The Ever-Open Door." People of all ages and at all stages of life, of all classes and kinds, some wearing costly robes, others in poverty-stricken raiment are portrayed at the threshold. Scientists are depicted laying aside their instruments, priests their crucifixes, ladies their jewels, and children their toys as they prepare to enter. The artist has most graphically illustrated his conception of the Door of Death.

Our Lord Jesus Christ has given us a far brighter outlook, for He came to depict the Door of Life, Himself the Passport who bids us enter in for security and salvation. This door is ever open because He ever lives. The figures of speech used of Him are startling and befit no other being in the universe, for He is called the living Bread, the living Way, the living Word, the living Stone. It would be equally correct to designate Him the living Door.

What a blessed picture this is of His beneficent grace, none other than the inconceivably glorious Jehovah deigning to appear in human form and becoming a door of entrance for His creature, man, so that the excluded be not exiled and the banished be not expelled for ever (2 Sam. 14:14). The path is open for man to pass out of the sphere of finite things and cross the threshold into a new realm where infinite realities are enjoyed evermore. Christ is the Door to a better country, a holy city of perfect peace, where evergreen pastures of pleasure and permanence abide, where the saved of the Lord may dwell in a paradise of perpetual purity, satisfied for ever. He is the Door of entrance to the haven of light effulgent, to the heritage of life abundant, and to the heaven of love transcendent.

We must needs remember that there can be no progress toward completion in the spiritual character and moral glory of our Saviour. No film of imperfection ever tarnished the brightness of that glory He had with the Father before the world was (John 17:5). We may say of Him as of no other, that in His character there is no room for improvement or increase, not one virtue could ever be bettered in Him, who is essentially and eternally "best." This should instill confidence into our hearts, forasmuch as it would be impossible to provide a better door for salvation than the one provided.

Three standpoints appear from whence we may view this salvation. Sometimes, in view of the completed action of deliverance wrought by the Lord Jesus, it is regarded as already past: "Not by works of righteousness which we have done, but according to His mercy He saved us" (Titus 3:5). At other times, having regard to the divine operation needed every moment to restrain from evil, it is spoken of as a present process: "Work out your own salvation with fear and trembling" (Phil. 2:12). We cannot work out a thing that we do not already possess. Then again, looking forward eagerly for the consummation which is alluded to as future, we are "kept by the power of God through faith unto salvation ready to be revealed in the last time" (1 Pet. 1:5). Yet withal entering this door has for its consequence eternal salvation. Christ is the Author of eternal salvation to all them that obey Him (Heb. 5:9). His sheep hear His voice and follow (John 10:3-4), therefore He gives unto them eternal life (John 10:28).

These separate aspects are welded into one harmonious

whole and may be comprehended in a glance that reaches back to the formation of the mighty plan before the ages, and reaches forward until it is lost in the infinitude of everlasting glory. What will it mean for these fetters of the flesh to be severed and for present boundaries to be burst asunder, that we may have a clear conception of eternal salvation! No other door in the knowledge of man opens to such fullness, vastness, and preciousness as this one does. "Except a man be born of water and of the Spirit, he cannot enter into the kingdom of God" (John 3:5). "I am the door: by Me if any man enter in, he shall be saved."

> The Cross of Christ is verily the key,
> By which our Saviour Lord
> Unlocked the door of immortality to you and me;
> And entering in Himself before,
> He set it wide for evermore;
> That we by His grace justified,
> And by His great love sanctified
> Might enter in all fearlessly
> And dwell forever by His side.
>
> J. OXENHAM

THE I AM OF INDIVIDUALITY

I am the good shepherd: the good shepherd giveth His life for the sheep. . . . I am the good shepherd, and know My sheep, and am known of Mine. As the Father knoweth Me, even so know I the Father: and I lay down My life for the sheep (John 10:11,14-15).

Let us be mindful that the speaker who here declares, "I am the good shepherd," is none other than the Creator Himself (John 1:3). For this reason the chapter is most startling, for it records that the immortal One who is incomprehensibly glorious, inconceivably gracious, and incomparably generous actually lays down His life for His loved ones. The expression, *layeth down,* is rendered in the A.V. *giveth* (verse 11), and the words *lay down* occur three times (verses 15,17,18). Primarily the expression indicates that He voluntarily offered Himself:

"No man taketh it from Me, but I lay it down of Myself." Positively, it intimates that He volitionally offered Himself: "I have power to lay it down." He willed to do it by firm resolve. Purposefully, He offered Himself vicariously: "I lay down my life *for* the sheep." Particularly, He offered Himself virtuously: the *good* shepherd layeth down his life. Prospectively, He offered Himself victoriously: "Therefore doth My Father love Me, because I lay down My life, that I may *take* it again." We are assured from Christ's clear statements that His death was not a mishap, much less a mistake. He had a perfect knowledge of the Father's will in the matter and was in full accord with His eternal counsels.

These five statements from our Lord's own lips certify His determined purpose to redeem His people by His own substitutionary death. In His detailed description of what His Shepherdhood involves, He virtually links the comeliness of His charming character, the completeness of His clear comprehension, the consciousness of His close companionship, and the changelessness of the covenant He was about to confirm with the glorious I AM title.

The shepherd needed by mankind had to have these celestial credentials, otherwise there could never have been a Saviour to deliver, "neither is there salvation in any other" (Acts 4:12). Furthermore, the present environment of those who appropriate this salvation demands an abiding shepherd that is able to defend his sheep against the attacks of the destroyer (John 10:10).

If we stop to consider the tempting enticements of the world that seduce, the thorny entanglements that surround, and the treacherous estrangements that smother loyalty and stifle love, His sheep require the strong sympathy and steadfast constancy of this precious Shepherd's tender care to shield and His good cheer to sustain under such conditions. We take delight in singing these choice lines:

> The King of love my Shepherd is,
> Whose goodness faileth never;
> I nothing lack if I am His,
> And He is mine forever.
> DORA GRENWELL

This Shepherd is a sovereign with authority to govern, He has supreme knowledge and is well qualified to guide, He has sufficient strength and as the almighty One will most assuredly guard His sheep. Yea He is permanent in His kingship, perfect in His knowledge, and patient in His kindness. His winsome Lordship and wise leadership are all that could be desired for safety, security, and satisfaction. We should bear in mind that when the Saviour affirmed that His sheep were given eternal life and would never perish, and that in His hand and His Father's hand they were absolutely secure, He was speaking in the presence of enemies (10:31).

How wonderfully interwoven His words were with Old Testament revelation. For instance, the psalm which is directed to the rock of our salvation combines creatorhood with shepherdhood and saviourhood as here. "In His hand are the deep places of the earth. . . . The sea is His, and He made it: and His hands formed the dry land. O come . . . let us kneel before the LORD our maker. For He is our God; and we are the people of His pasture, and the sheep of His hand" (Ps. 95:4-7).

With such a celebrity as our Caretaker, whose shepherdlike constancy, competency, and chivalry are unimpeachable, let us rest contentedly in the truthfulness of His sayings, let us rejoice complacently in the tenderness of His sympathy, let us rely confidently on the tirelessness of His strength, and let us revel continually in the trustworthiness of His superior knowledge.

THE I AM OF INDESTRUCTIBILITY

> Jesus saith unto her, Thy brother shall rise again. Martha saith unto Him, I know that he shall rise again in the resurrection at the last day. Jesus said to her, I am the resurrection, and the life (John 11:23-25).

In the three preceding Gospels we are furnished with a perfect picture of Christ's activities; whereas John, with his contemplative insight, conducts us to a vantage point from whence we may view the inner glories of our Saviour's wondrous life. This startling claim of Christ is connected with the seventh sign recorded by John, each one of which signs is a specific symbol of heavenly realities. John initiates us into seeing the more important moral features which lie behind the physical phenomena. He marshals these signs, which are object lessons for inculcating spiritual truth, and presents them in a suggestive logical sequence, from the marriage gladness in Cana of Galilee to the mortuary sadness in Bethany of Judea.

We are introduced to One in the midst of mankind who is able to transform water into wine, translate from darkness to light, and transfigure death into life, who is none other than the great I AM. *I* stands for personality, while *AM* signifies presence; so the prevalence of the Lord's personal presence is age-abiding. He ever was and is and will be. This is He who never leaves and never forsakes; He never departs and never deserts, but is always ever present, eternally. Surely there is nothing incredible about the raising of the dead by a person of such caliber. "I am the resurrection" is followed by the words, "and the life." The force of this means that Christ is the Life of those whom He raises from death. Such a claim well befits the lips of the Creator, by whom all things were made (John 1:3).

Our Lord speaks on this occasion in the calm consciousness of one who possesses the majestic might that wields mastery over the mysterious monster, death. The dark gloom of that ugly fortress no longer terrifies; our Saviour has power over all the power of the enemy. One mighty Champion has arisen who has conquered the Goliath of the grave, one master Personality has prevailed gloriously over the grim and ghoulish enemy, death. With what sympathy of heart, sovereignty of spirit, and supremacy of will He approached with the sisters the tomb in Bethany, to demonstrate the reality of the unprecedented claim He had made. In a clear, strong voice He uttered His command and Lazarus came forth, an ever-reverberating witness to all the world and all its generations that what He had said earlier would certainly transpire, when at a coming hour all that are in the graves would hear His voice and come forth (John 5:28-29).

Even greater confirmation than this was given, for when men sought with violence to destroy His body, He Himself entered death's domain, emerging the third day in all the majesty of an invincible life.

The resurrection of Christ is monumental in history as a worthy triumph to celebrate, and is also fundamental in prophecy as a worthy topic to contemplate (Acts 2:24-31). The Scriptural record we possess of this sensational event confirms faith, convinces reason, creates hope, and coronates power. Therefore Christ risen causes wonder and constrains worship. Yea, a risen Christ is the Pledge of resurrection authority (Eph. 1:19-20), the Proof of coming harvest (1 Cor. 15:20), the Power of an endless life (Heb. 7:10,25), the Pattern of the believer's new life (Rom. 6:4,11), and the Pledge of our justification (Acts 13:39). So the grave with its grief is not the final goal. He who is full of grace and truth has given to us a glimpse of the ultimate by demonstrating the glory of God, as being Himself the resurrection and the life. The stately sublimity of such power assures the permanent stability of His kingdom of everlasting righteousness.

THE I AM OF INSUPERABILITY

Jesus saith unto him, I am the way, the truth, and the life: no man cometh unto the Father, but by Me (John 14:6).

The realized fullness of divine revelation depends on the recognition of the fullness of human need, and there is no more sriking example of this than that which is presented in the revealed Name of the One who is the basis of all being, the mystical I AM. Initially, the truth is stated in an absolute manner, from the point of view of divine fullness and essence, and without limitation whatsoever, "I AM THAT I AM" (Ex. 3:14).

Standing by itself the title is unintelligible, human reason is lost in trying to traverse such infinitudes of incalculable sufficiency. It is as though the boundless ocean attempted to tell of its imponderable immensity to a tiny crab stranded on the shore. The character of the Name implies: I am the constant One, consistently without conclusion; I am the changeless One, changelessly without cessation; and I am the administering One, continuously without consummation.

The ever-abiding revelation of the Name started with the statement of a fact which is absolute, and that leaves the mind bewildered, astounded, and unsatisfied. But as the course of history spread out and made real the lesson of man's failure, which it does most assuredly, the same history taught also the lesson of man's need. Man eventually came to realize the failure and to recognize the need. A vast vacuum was formed into which came the influx of God's revealed truth. The revelation which at first appeared shapeless and illimitable began gradually and practically to take a definite form. God so acted that His divine grace became adapted to human need. He spoke to enslaved Israel and said "I am Jehovah your God, who bringeth you out from under the burden of the Egyptians" (Ex. 6:7 ASV). To an emancipated people sorely stricken He said, "I am Jehovah that healeth thee" (Ex. 15:26 ASV). To an endangered ruler harassed by foes He said, "I am thy salvation" (Ps. 35:3). To an ensnared nation defiled by sin He said, "I am Jehovah, your Holy One. . . . I . . . am He that blotteth out thy transgressions for Mine own sake" (Is. 43:15, 25). So the I AM wields the prerogatives to deliver, heal, save, and justify.

When the fullness of time was come and man's disaffection of heart and anguish of spirit had become intensified and his need of intervention was the more keenly felt, God spoke again through His Son, born of a woman, so that His very Word of verity became incarnate. This time I AM meets every need of the human race. We cannot see salvation, look upon love, gaze upon grace, or perceive purity save as they take bodily form and are demonstrated by expressive action in a living personality. If the eternal I AM, the Basis of all being, the Originator of entity, the Creator and Maker of all things is to become a constant power and constraining motive in the life of mankind, humanity must be able to observe Him at work in manifestation among men, as Man in the image of God.

Wherefore the I AM "became flesh and dwelt among us" says John, and we beheld His glory, heard His voice, believed His Word, and received His grace.

There can be no mistaking His identity; His claims were clear and explicit. "I am the bread of life," "I am the light of the world," "I am the door: by Me if any man enter in, he shall be saved," "I am the good shepherd," "I am the son of God," "I am the resurrection," "I am the way, the truth, and the life." Here we discover that food, light, leadership, liberty, and every vital necessity are freely and fully met by the infinite, eternal, and unchangeable Christ. So simply, calmly, and yet most majestically, our Lord claims to be the Son, Saviour, Shepherd, and Sustainer, yea, the One who is able to conquer death, forgive sin, save the soul, slake thirst, and satisfy the heart forever more, to the glory of God the Father.

Humanitarian views of Christ which cherish thoughts of Him as man and martyr, extolling the beauty of His character and eulogizing the benignity of His care and compassion are wont to balk at this point and utterly break down. At this stage the blessed Lord was standing on the brink of the beyond and had brought the matter of His departure to the attention of His disciples. Uncertainty as to their ever finding the traceless, trackless highway gripped them. In response to the objections of Thomas, who asked what every sensible person asks sooner or later, "How can we know the way?" He answered, "I am the way, the truth, and the life."

When we stop to contemplate the Father's house, the fadeless kingdom, the holy habitation, the deathless domain, and the glorious heritage of the saints in light, we should certainly be moved to inquire the way to reach such a realm of bliss. Men of modern thought make many suggestions and advocate as a means of approach such things as a sincere desire to do good, earnest endeavor, regard for religious rites, philanthropy, humanitarianism, traditionalism, universalism, the way of orthodoxy, ethical aspiration, sentimental aestheticism, and scores of other means of attaining the desired haven. Christ indicates that all of these means are unavailing, and declares most decidedly, "I am the way . . . no man cometh unto the Father, but by Me." He plainly taught there were only two ways for man to choose: the one which leads to life everlasting, and the other which ends in destruction.

Our Lord, by His reassuring voice of certitude delivers us from the labyrinth of theoretical deductions by affirming emphatically, "I am the way." If we recall the character of the One we have sought to trace in these pages, we shall do well to consider His challenging claim, for He has a right to speak. Let us not resent the sublime simplicity of His teaching, which so simplifies the whole matter of salvation, but rather let us receive the truth and thank Him for clarifying the otherwise obscure problem, while at the same time we ourselves avail ourselves of the provided access.

The Old Testament records the way of life: the way of righteousness, the way of peace, the way of holiness, and such like. All of these have been centered in one Person, for Christ as the Way is our Life, Righteousness, Peace, and Holiness. We must needs repair to Him, receive Him, repose in Him, revere His teaching, and rejoice in His matchless goodness. Christ is the one complete Way to the Father, He is the whole Truth of that Way, and He is the entire Life of that Way that leads to light and liberty eternal.

THE I AM OF INSEPARABILITY

I am the true vine, and My Father is the husbandman. . . . I am the vine, ye are the branches: he that abideth in Me, and I in him, the same bringeth forth much fruit (John 15:1,5).

In the first section of John's message, our Lord selected the figure of a springing well and flowing stream to set forth the fullness and felicities of the Spirit of life with its unction. In chapters 8 to 12, where He claims to be the Light of the world, He states that the inevitable outcome would result in one flock and one Shepherd, for light obviously leads to unity. The closing section is occupied mainly with His love, and the metaphor chosen to represent this feature is the vine and the branches, for love promotes union. These three matchless figures in combination express the endless resources of life, the eclipseless radiance of light, and the exhaustless reserves of love, which are resident in Christ the Creator. This being so, and having stated His I AM claim in conjunction with the vine, He immediately added the words, without Me ye can do nothing" (verse 5).

We are fully aware that the age-abiding I AM can do everything, make anything He pleases, and create all things He determines. Wherefore, if His people are to glorify His name in spiritual fruitbearing of unrivaled quality and unlimited quantity, union with Him is absolutely and vitally essential. What possibility is there for divine love, joy, grace, peace, virtue, vitality, and suchlike to flourish without Him? The union is primarily for affection; love is spoken of ten times in the chapter. The union is purposefully entered for production; fruit is referred to eight times. The union is picturesquely emphasized for a function; the term *abide*—both "in me" and "in the vine"—is used eight times. The union is participatingly entered into for expression; "Herein is My Father glorified." "Greater works than these shall [ye] do" (14:12); the term *greater* occurs twelve times in John's Gospel.

Apart from the virtuous sap and vigorous strength, the branch cannot bear fruit of itself. The wondrous love, in its immensity subsisting between Father and Son, is here brought into prominence to brighten the prospect of productiveness (verse 8). The personal love of Christ is the greatest exhilarating and stimulating potency to constrain effort and contribute energy that has ever been revealed. How impressively the Lord imprinted the importance of His virtuous love on the minds of His disciples (verse 10). His amazing claim, "I am the true vine," is full of infinite significance, for, embedded in His words, inestimable spiritual treasures lie concealed. His sayings are like a garden of spices, a spring shut up, a fountain sealed (S. of Sol. 4:12). New beauties, new benefits, and new blessings are constantly emerging from the gracious words He spoke, which are ever fresh and fragrant. The dignity of His life and the divinity of His love supply vigor and virtue to the branches, resulting in luscious clusters of spiritual fruit. By the luminosity of His light, the generosity of His grace, and the notoriety of His Name, what excellent production is assured to gratify the Father's heart and glorify His honor.

Let us bear in mind that oneness is the great objective of His omnipotent will. The signal symbolism Christ selected to illustrate His transcendent teaching expresses a living unction, a lasting unity, and a loving union (John 7:39; 10:16; 15:5). This main trend of His ministry is likewise obvious when we consider the focal point of His famous prayer, "That they all may be *one;* as Thou, Father, art in Me, and I in Thee, that they also may be *one* in Us: that the world may believe that Thou hast sent Me. And the glory which Thou gavest Me I have given them; that they may be *one,* even as We are *one* . . . and that the world may know that Thou hast sent Me, and hast loved them, as Thou hast loved Me" (John 17:21-23). Remember that the unanimity, uniformity, and unity emphasized in this unique utterance express the ultimate objective which underlies the purpose of Christ's manifestation as Redeemer, His ministration as Regenerator, and His mediation as Reconciler.

Christ linked His credentials and capabilities with the prerogatives and potentialities centered in the celebrated Name with which He fully identified Himself. While advancing to the close of His earthly ministry, He assured His disciples that His priceless Name is the perfect pledge of all the precious promises, the present proof of His perpetual presence, and the potent plea in all prevailing prayer.

As we continue to increase in the knowledge of Him, His Name becomes more fragrant to memory, more jubilant to praise, and more radiant to hope. We may have learned to revel in the renowned names of patriarchs whom we greatly revere, or dwell with fond memories on the famous names of notable pioneers and discoverers, or boast in the honored names of philanthropists that we have come to admire, or recall the princely heroes who have reinstated an imperiled freedom, but standing highest and ranking noblest is the Name above every name. A very unusual significance is attached to His unique Name, which the gliding centuries cannot crowd out from holding the most conspicuous place in the annals of history.

Revelation assures us that the celestial confines of the remote heavens reverberate with their unceasing contribution of praise to His enduring Name. The great concourse of Christian congregations joins constantly in worship in order to commemorate the high honors of His everlasting Name. The gracious constancy and capability centered in His Name minister cheer and comfort the world over to multitudes of needy hearts. His immortal Name carries with it supreme merit in majesty and mediatorial mercy, bears the noblest claims of constancy and crowning consistency, offers the surest pledge of promise and plenteous provision, commands the greatest rights of resource and replete riches, ranks foremost in its fame of faithfulness and friendly fellowship, stands preeminent in power to prevail and in perfecting peace, and holds the heaviest weight of worthiness and wondrous witness universally. Engirdled by a golden circlet of love His Name scintillates its radiance as the sunlight in every region round about, expanding in ever-widening horizons of God-honoring helpfulness.

As we listen to the broadcast with rapt attention, we hear the words, "Whosoever shall call on the name of the Lord shall be saved"; "Whatsoever ye shall ask of the Father in My name He [will] give it you"; "For where two or three are gathered together in My name, there am I in the midst"; "What things soever ye desire, when ye pray," and so forth.

How frequently we find the lifeless treasures of a long lost lover being seduously cared for and kept scrupulously clean by a bereaved companion. But what are we doing to fulfill the command of our living, loving, thrice-blessed Lord? Are the things that are dear to Him dear to us? Are those interests most precious to Him, still precious to us? Is the work He delights to see done, a real delight for us to do?

Glorious as are the values of his Name thus far, we should be prepared for greater marvels and magnitudes in the final unveiling which He imparted to John in Patmos.

THE I AM OF INIMITABILITY

The Apocalypse, or unveiling of Jesus Christ, from which revelation the essence and substance of our entire volume is derived, lays special stress on the personal priority and perpetual preeminence of Jesus Christ our Lord. All the majestic portrayals displayed in the symbolic visions of His final revelation are beheld and described from a heavenly standpoint. The events and experiences encountered by the Church and the bond servants on earth in the executing of the Great Commission are seen in the light of an enthroned Christ, exalted at the right hand of the Majesty on high. The word *throne* is referred to forty-five times in the book.

Gloriously environed in supernal splendor, our dignified Lord now lifts the great claims and names of His deity to the highest altitudes of the most spacious sovereignty conceivable, so that they transcend the utmost bound of human comprehension. The I AMs previously uttered at the time of Israel's emancipation from Egypt, and those voiced by Christ during the manifestation, are here elevated to a nameless degree of supernatural stateliness. The first of these proclamations from the lips of the ascended and glorified Lord is amazing in its range of regency and standard of sublimity.

> I am Alpha and Omega, the beginning and the ending, saith the Lord, which is, and which was, and which is to come, the Almighty (Rev. 1:8).

Such fascinating figures of speech denote that He is the foremost in precedence, the uppermost in preeminence, and the uttermost in permanence. In fact the widest range of authority and farthest reach of administration are included in this inimitable claim. The spacious splendors incorporated in the acclamation are too vast in their magnitude for our human minds to visualize. Our calculations are cramped and curtailed within the limited confines of the finite, whereas His powers and prerogatives are ageless, limitless, and measureless, because He is infinite in His capacity, capability, and continuity, for He can never be suspended, succeeded, or superseded. He is the Commencer and Consummator of all revelation as the Alpha and Omega; He is the Originator and Objective of all creation as the Beginning and Ending; and He is the Promoter and Perfecter of all administration as the One which is, and which was, and which is to come, the Almighty.

Although we cannot venture very far into the vastness of these three widespread vocations, let us at least state a surface feature of each of His most worthy offices. Christ is the incorruptible Foundation who will synchronize all, for all things are to be gathered together in one (Eph. 1:10). He is the imperishable Fullness to standardize all, "that they may be one, even as We are one" (John 17:21, see also Eph. 4:5). He is also the impregnable Fastness to stabilize all, for in that day there shall be one Lord and His name one (Zech. 14:9).

So we are exhorted by the prophet, in those well-known words, to trust in the Lord forever, for in the Rock of ages is everlasting strength. Christ is the incorruptible Foundation of all things visible and invisible, both of the manifest and the mysterious, of the revealed and of the concealed, of the obvious and of the obscure, of the material and of the spiritual, of the terrestrial and of the celestial, of the temporal and of the eternal. "Other foundation can no man lay than that is laid, which is Jesus Christ" (1 Cor. 3:11). In the light of this, can we not recognize that all things are naked and open unto the eyes of Him with whom we have to do?

Christ is the imperishable Fullness, to sustain and maintain, to renew and restore, to govern and guide, to decree and direct, to supervise and stabilize, to establish and abolish, to advocate and adjudicate, to seek and to save, to pardon and punish, to redeem and reconcile, to upraise and uphold, to judge and to justify, to create and regenerate, for of His fullness have all we received and grace for grace.

He is the impregnable Fastness for sodality and stability, forever alive and alert, delivering and defending His people, shielding and sustaining His redeemed, controlling and consoling His saints, while centralizing and supervising all worship in a perfected kingdom.

The two vowels He uses, *Alpha* and *Omega,* which occur in the great title *Jehovah* in Hebrew, appear 7,600 times in the Old Testament. The three tenses, present, past, and future, as the commencement and climax of all regal title, legal claim, and moral right defy exposition. He is the same in name and fame forever, without variableness and shadow of turning, reigning and remaining the glorious and gracious Sovereign-Shepherd everlastingly. Such prodigious claims as these were never made by any one before or since; yet every syllable befits His personal character, who is "faithful and true."

For any other claimant to utter such words would be preposterous. Christ borrowed no flame from the sun, He created it; and He derived no fame from human sources, for He made mankind. Essentially, He has the truest of titles; He owns the divinest of authentic deeds; He voices the clearest of imperishable claims; He holds the rarest of unassailable rights; He bears the noblest of precious names; He sways the strongest of sovereign scepters; and He wears the comeliest of celestial crowns. The personal glories of Christ baffle all our human conceptions of grandeur, while His splendor staggers the comprehension of the greatest intellect.

> To whom then will ye liken Me, or shall I be equal? saith the Holy One. Lift up your eyes on high, and behold who hath created these things, that bringeth out their host by number: He calleth them all by names by the greatness of His might, for that He is strong in power: not one faileth (Is. 40:25-26).

THE I AM OF INEXHAUSTIBILITY

> I was in the Spirit on the Lord's day, and heard behind me a great voice, as of a trumpet, saying, I am Alpha and Omega, the first and the last (Rev. 1:10-11).

The Lord's Day *(kuriakee)* is a continuous testimony to the Lord's triumph over death (verse 5), and is followed by the trophies gained in conquest, namely, the keys of hell and of death (verse 18). The use that is made here of *Lord's* as an adjective occurs in only one other instance in the New Testa-

ment, in which case the Lord's supper is mentioned (1 Cor.
11:20). This fact excludes the passage from being used as
referring to the day of the Lord as in 2 Peter 3:10, where we
meet with *Tee hemera keriou*. God has established a witness to
the triumph of Christ's resurrection, which is commemorated
fifty-two times a year by virtue of the Lord's Day. In addition
to the abiding testimony to the triumph, the tokens also were
stated by the risen Christ Himself to be in His possession; for
He declared He had the trophy of His victory in the keys which
He held securely.

We have already dealt, in *The Indescribable Christ*, with
the limitless conceptions of measureless capacity and capability which are involved in the credentials of Christ as the Alpha
and Omega. He is the Fullness of the divine subsistence, the
Sum and Substance of the divine thought, speech, wisdom,
and reason, the very Exegete of the Eternal, the Exhibition of
essential truth, the Essence of excellence in Godhead, the full
Expression of the everlasting Word. On first thought, it appears incredible that the intricacies and niceties of innumerable subjects, events, narratives, feelings, experiences,
histories, poems, records, biographies, autobiographies,
sciences, laws, and suchlike, in all their multiform variety, can
be tabulated through the medium of words formed from the
twenty-six letters contained in the alphabet.

More astounding than this is the fact that the revelation of
the infinities of Godhead, the incorruptible features of everlasting life, love, and light; the immortal fullness of grace,
peace, and mercy; the imperishable forces of creative power,
controlling might, and ceaseless strength; the ineffable
fairness of beauty, purity, integrity, and constancy; the impregnable foundations of righteousness, goodness, meekness,
and holiness; the inestimable functions of mediation, redemption, regeneration, and reconciliation; the inexhaustible fountains of salvation, sustentation, sanctification, and satiation;
the indestructible fruits and fragrance of spiritual sacrifice,
suffering, submission, and service; and a myriad more indispensable faculties and facilities are all resident in the person of Jesus Christ, for in Him dwelleth all the fullness of

Godhead bodily, and from Him we receive life and breath and all things — and that is true of over four thousand million of the world's population at the present hour — for He is all and in all, the Lord of lords and King of kings.

Everything about Him is superlatively superhuman and supernatural. How tiny a portion of His immensities we conceive and how small a section of His immutabilities we comprehend. His vigor, His vision, His voice, and His vocation will be found to excel exceedingly and everlastingly everywhere, as disclosed in the verses that follow this titanic claim. Therefore, the venerable maturity of Christ's majesty is without parallel, the vast sovereignty of His world-wide dominion is without equal, while the virtuous nobility of His nature stands without rival.

THE I AM OF INVINCIBILITY

And when I saw Him, I fell at His feet as dead. And He laid His right hand upon me, saying unto me, Fear not; I am the first and the last (Rev. 1:17).

Every detail of Christ's ministry here on earth is dignified and desirable, but every display of His majesty in Heaven expresses dignity multiplied and desirability magnified. When John the apostle beheld his Master glorified, he was overawed and overcome by the overwhelming sight. As we advance in the knowledge of our Lord Jesus Christ and reach a more adequate apprehension of His adorable attributes, the only appropriate attitude is that of reverential awe.

The twelvefold presentation of Christ in the context accounts for this abject prostration of the bond servant. Our present capacities are too frail to stand even a single flash of His eternal weight of glory, let alone a full view of it. John saw his majestic Master magnificent in might as Son of man, resplendent in righteousness, clothed with a garment down to the foot, vibrant in virtue, girt about the breasts with a golden girdle, inerrant in intelligence; His head and His hair were white like wool, as white as snow; prescient in perception, His eyes were as a flame of fire; jubilant in justice, His feet were like unto fine brass as if they burned in a furnace; competent in command, His voice was as the sound of many waters; radiant in royalty, He had in His right hand seven stars; triumphant in truth, out of His mouth went a sharp two-edged sword; brilliant in beauty, His countenance was as the sun shineth in its strength; lambent in light, when John saw Him he fell at His feet as dead, munificent in mercy, and He laid His right hand upon John, salient in sympathy, saying, "Fear not; I am the first and the last." Little wonder the well-beloved apostle wondered with awe-struck veneration and worshiped with all his heart and mind and soul.

We should recall that the earliest use of this claim of being the First and the Last appears in the message of Isaiah the prophet. John at the time of his vision was on the isle called Patmos. In the verse following the declarations in Isaiah, the prophet says, "The isles saw . . . and feared" (Is. 41:5). The fear there, as here, is allayed by assurance of help from the I AM (Is. 41:10; 13:14). In chapter 44 the declaration is more spacious and specific: "Thus saith Jehovah, the King of Israel, and his Redeemer, Jehovah of hosts; I am the first, and I am the last; and beside Me there is no God" (Is. 44:6). The "fear not" again appears with the assurance of being chosen witnesses against idolatry (Is. 44:2,8).

Great comfort is to be derived from Christ's claiming to be the First and the Last. In this capacity He outlives all idolatrous opposition and all iniquitous oppression. They who inflict penalties on His people and imprison His servants and saints must needs succumb to His enduring sovereignty. So this title is definitely directed to help and hearten John in his banishment. He proves that his Lord and Master is wholly familiar with the pressure of circumstances to which he has been subjected because of his witness. Why be afraid when the almighty One says, "Fear not; I am the first and the last." Why fear sin? The sinless One atones adequately. Why fear life? The living One lives and loves abidingly. Why fear death? The risen deathless One ascends triumphantly. Why fear the beyond? The exalted One assures convincingly. Why fear the ages? The ageless One administers immortally. Why fear foes?

The enthroned One rules and reigns eternally. Why fear defects? The spotless One avails perfectly. Yea, verily, we are altogether accepted in the Beloved, everlastingly.

Christ's name and fame as the First and the Last cover the whole wide range of realism; indicating that He is the Sum and Substance from start to finish, the Fountain and Fullness from spring to sea, the Origin and Objective from gateway to goal, yea, the Framer in priority and Finisher in finality of all things. We need our thoughts of Him to be enlarged, expanded, and exalted, until He fills and thrills our hearts with loftier conceptions of His transcendent glory. We should resolve to take a more attentive look at His lofty lordship as Son of man, recall afresh that this dignified Lover "loved us and loosed us from our sins by His own blood," and then learn anew to admire and adore His intrinsic loveliness, by virtue of which we shall long to live and labor for Him alone. If we rate His love highly, we shall be stirred to ardent activity, our gratitude will grow deeper, our devotion stronger, and our loyalty firmer.

> Look! ye saints, the sight is glorious,
>   See the Man of Sorrows now,
> From the fight returned victorious:
>   Every knee to Him shall bow.
> Crown Him! Crown Him!
>   Crowns become the Victor's brow.
> THOMAS KELLY

THE I AM OF IMMORTALITY

I am . . . the Living one; and I became dead, and behold, I am alive for evermore, and I have the keys of death and of Hades (Rev. 1:18 ASV).

What accents of authority arrest our attention here, what syllables of sovereignty sound forth in martial strain, what soul-thrilling tones of triumph reecho grandly in His wondrous words, "Behold, I am alive forevermore," and with an authority that is paramount for the protection and preservation of His people. A majestic hand of might and mercy holds the master keys.

Whatever the estimate we may place on the witness of the apostles to the resurrection, the chief corroboration and crowning confirmation to assure that Christ overcame death come from the Conqueror Himself, after His coronation at God's right hand. We cannot speak of neutral tints here; there is nothing trivial in the display; every word the risen Christ utters is regal, vital, and final. Notice particularly the change of rendering in the American Standard Version. The Authorized Version reads "was dead," which is passive and refers to a past state; "became dead" is active, and refers to a personal act. Christ affirmed in John's record that He had power to lay down His life and power to take it again, adding, as He did so, that no one had taken it from Him. In the truest sense, Christ's death was His own volitional act; He gave Himself (Titus 2:14). He now appends the rare nobility and royal dignity of the richest name, I AM, to His glory-life in a resurrection reign, where He is in possession of the keys of hell and death.

Our Lord bears many marks of majestic sovereignty, every one of which contributes weighty evidence in confirmation of His stalwart superiority and stately supremacy. The manifold variety of His exclusive qualities towers loftily above those of all other distinguished celebrities combined, none of whom were capable of mastering death and of mitigating its sorrows on man's behalf. The devil is now a defeated foe, his palace is disgorged of captives, and death itself is doomed to destruction (1 Cor. 15:26). By virtue of Christ's victory over the forces of evil, He does not alarm His servants, but assures them; He never confuses, but comforts; He will not compel, but constrains; and to those who are agitated and afraid, He still speaks His kindly words in kingly tone, "Fear not, I am He."

Let us listen often and attentively to our beloved Lord as He declares Himself in these deathless words: "I am He that liveth . . . and, behold, I am alive for evermore." So by His conquest of death, He brought life and immortality to light. In the durable domain of His everlasting dominion, He will ever delight to display to His redeemed hosts the battle dress of sacrifice in which He fought the foe and triumphed. Throughout the glorious panorama of this unveiling, He presents Himself as the Lamb, that sacrificial character in which He conquered the arch-adversary and his infernal forces. A very uncommon distinction environs the victory of our valiant Lord and Commander-in-Chief, for in His going forth to battle He did not approach the field of conflict with the stentorian roar of the lion, but with the silent reticence of the Lamb (Is. 53:7).

The values of His victory survive the centuries because its virtues cannot be localized by any one race, nor nationalized by any people; its purpose is universal for all mankind to believe in and rejoice constantly.

The resurrection of Christ is the most colossal of all conquests, the most venerable of all victories, and the most tremendous triumph ever gained in any realm. The prophet Daniel in his day was overawed by the vision he beheld of the solitary Son of man in regal sovereignty, subduing the mighty kingdoms of men that were characterized by the most ferocious representations of brute force. He saw these fade from the earth in the presence of the majestic mastery of Messiah, who will return and abolish all tyranny and establish the absolute authority of His everlasting dominion.

THE I AM OF ILLIMITABILITY

And He that sat upon the throne said, Behold, I make all things new. And He said unto me, Write: for these words are true and faithful. And He said unto me, It is done. I am Alpha and Omega, the beginning and the end. I will give unto him that is athirst of the fountain of the water of life freely (Rev. 21:5-6).

Well nigh two thousand years have passed since the Lord announced to John His unprecedented purpose to make all things new, and straightway from His steadfast throne He commissioned the apostle to write the words of His proclamation, for "these," said He, "are true and faithful." We know of no other potentate whose words retain their authority through all the centuries and whose limitless prerogatives and boundless potentialities are altogether immune from mortality. Need we wonder that no word of His can fruitless fall, for we hear ringing clearly, sounding loudly, and echoing grandly, the age-old and world-wide declaration of His memorable and memorial name, I AM.

What an amazing array of wonders is witnessed in this chapter! Who but the I AM of the ages could plan and pursue a purpose to establish a perfect society such as the one indicated in the City of God. Let us recall the fact that "I am Alpha and Omega" is the Repository of reason, the Reservoir of resource, and the Revealer of reality, who determines to make known to principalities and powers in heavenly places the manifold wisdom of God. With the resources of His unsearchable riches He can do unspeakable things, and this eternal Architect of the everlasting ages has designedly purposed to construct the edifice of a perfect society, comprised of living stones as a spiritual house for His own holy habitation. The tabernacle, temple, and throne of the Almighty mentioned in this chapter will be established in the midst of an innumerable multitude of glorified saints, each of whom bears the character of the Redeemer and Regenerator; each one of whom is conformed to His image in purity, beauty, integrity, and glory. What a resemblance! Forasmuch as by virtue of His foreordained counsels He laid the foundation of this society as the First, He is well able to finish the construction and consolidate the social security of His saints forever, because He is the Last.

The marvels of His electing love, the magnificence of His emancipating power, and the munificence of His exceeding grace will then be more fully grasped and enjoyed. In this embellished estate of permanent paradise, environed with the embattlements of everlasting righteousness, we shall see His enduring Name emblazoned in glowing colors and drenched in sweetest perfume, to enhance the enlightenment, enrichment, and enjoyment of the hosts of His purified people, to whom He is so endeared by virtue of what He is in Himself. His primeval covenant of constancy as the great I AM is not an idle dream but a predetermined, immutable ideal.

When this designed objective is reached, the glorious

mystery of the divine love, the gracious majesty of His desirable loveliness, and the generous mercy of His devoted labor will be recognized and their priceless values realized and revered. Then we shall be introduced to the fruits of His unlimited vitality, to the friendship of His unrivaled fidelity, to the fervor of His unchanging constancy, to the features of His unblemished beauty, to the fellowship of His unbounded society, to the fullness of His unsullied glory, and to the fragrance of His untarnished Name.

"Who in the skies can be compared unto Jehovah? Who among the sons of the mighty is like unto Jehovah? A God very terrible in the council of the holy ones, and to be feared above all them that are about Him" (Ps. 89:6-7 ASV). No one but the I AM could produce a society so perfect in symmetry, so exquisite in beauty, so immaculate in purity, and so radiant in glory, as that signified in the City of God. There all tears dry, tombs vanish, thorns perish, troubles cease, trials end, turmoil dies, and the tranquility of a complacent calm pervades immortally.

> He ever was and is to be,
> The First and Last who set us free.
> Launched in the Godhead's widest sea,
> We're lost in love's immensity.
>
> C. J. R.

THE I AM OF INFINITY

I am Alpha and Omega, the beginning and the end, the first and the last (Rev. 22: 13).

At this point we come to the supreme summit and reach the sublime climax of claim. This triple title envelops a whole world of wonders; for Christ, in the use He makes here of these designations, spans three dimensions in realms that to man are undefinable. No words ever framed are so famous, no standard of superiority ever conceived is so spacious, and no degree of dignity ever expressed is so glorious in repleteness of range and regality, as our Lord stipulates here. In this self-revelation of His own character as Chief Executor, Christ reaffirms the exclusive distinction He holds as standing without equal or rival, Himself the Revealer, the Creator, and the Redeemer. Every important title, every imperial office, and every indispensable vocation is included and incorporated within the bounds of this magnificent declaration. Every realm is involved, every right is implied, and every resource is indicated most graphically.

In making this sublime statement of claim, Christ figuratively identifies Himself as the One who originated all things, and fully interprets His far-reaching functions as the Ordainer and Overseer of administrative authority. He vouches by these words, that He is the Founder and foremost Source of virtue and vision, the Framer and the Fullness in subsistence of vitality and volition, and the Finisher who is the final sequence as Vindicator and Victor, the One who vanquishes the devil and death and verifies the eternal purpose of God.

This personal description which Christ gives to us of His own inherent capacities and infinite resources marks Him out as being the sole Reservoir and Revealer of truth, a fact that He couples with the alphabet, which is a figure of endless sufficiency and also forcefully suggests His finality, symbolizes His adaptability, signifies His superiority, stipulates His immutability, and sets forth substantially His very deity. Christ Himself is the personal Embodiment of truth, the Essence of its correctness, and the living Expression of its effulgent wisdom. Wherefore, there is no phase of truth's many facets which He does not enhance. By virtue of His immaculate character He beautifies meekness, He enriches goodness, He ornaments greatness, He guilds preciousness, He burnishes loving-kindness, He perfumes sweetness, He adorns righteousness, He embellishes graciousness, He amplifies worthiness, He engraces winsomeness, He magnifies holiness, and glorifies perfectness.

As Beginning and End, Christ is foremost in priority and therefore precedes by the character of His own personality everything conceivable. He is the Beginning of light effulgent, power omnipotent, truth translucent, knowledge omniscient, grace abundant, love transparent, life sentient, and peace permanent, all of which emanate from Him, for He is the Embodiment of all the fullness of God. A complete celestial constellation of superlative sublimities could only prove inadequate when endeavoring to describe such a personality. The remoteness of Christ's renown, the range of His resource, the rank of His regality, the realm of His reign, and the riches of His glory out-measure all the capacities of human conception. Little wonder that He said during His ministry on earth, "No man knoweth who the Son is" (Luke 10:22). After the patriarch Job had rehearsed to his august friends a few facts of the marvels of creation, he exclaimed, "Lo, these are but the outskirts of His ways: And how small a whisper do we hear of Him" (Job 26:14 ASV).

In addition to His being the sole Source and Originator of all things visible and invisible, thrones and dominions, principalities and powers, Christ is also the End. That is, He is the Terminus of truth, the triple Crown of all verity, the scintillating radiance and superb resplendence of reality. Mercy likewise finds its majestic monarch in Messiah, who is forever matchless in His full-orbed magnificence. Love also ends with Him, for He magnified the generosity of love by giving Himself, the precious Prince of life, as a Sacrifice to save. Power, too, is final in Him, who, as the almighty One, sways the glorious scepter of control in Heaven and earth unceasingly. He is the Climax of constancy and fidelity in His indestructible priestly ministry, in which capacity He is perfected forevermore. He is the true Goal of grace, the crystal Fountain, the continual Fullness, and the consummate Finality of both glory and beauty. Christ as the End is the Sum total of spotless righteousness, the Zenith of sterling goodness and the Perfection of steadfast holiness. These factors find their full complement in His exquisite character.

Considering such matters negatively, Christ puts an end to all trials, tears, tragedies, and terrors. Positively, He is the End of all virtuous excellence and vital perfection, in that these attributes find their completion in Him entirely and eternally.

Wherefore we may confidently say that in magnitude of might, in plenitude of power, in amplitude of authority, in rectitude of right, in certitude of claim, in aptitude of ability, and in fortitude of strength, He is beyond compare. Are we surprised, in contemplating such divinely noble qualities, that He should be the only One in the presence of three worlds accounted worthy to take the title deeds of the entire universe? (Rev. 5)

Let us dwell more frequently on the riches of His plenteous grace, precious gifts, spacious government, and lustrous glory, for these outvie, outrange, and outlast the ages of the ages. Therefore, the End, by interpretation, is the essential Entity, the presiding Personality, the deathless Deity, who is over all, God blessed forever (Rom. 9:5).

No wonder the most brilliant of the scholars under the tutelage of Gamaliel, the philosopher of Palestine, after he had experienced regeneration, burst forth in exclamation saying, "O the depth of the riches both of the wisdom and knowledge of God! how unsearchable are His judgments, and His ways past finding out!" (Rom. 11:33)

How impossible it is for us to advance any further into this mysterious reserve of multiform greatness. Yet, one other registered gateway does stand open for access, in that Christ says for the fifth time in this closing book, "I am the first and the last." What an insight this gives of His activities in relation to the great essential achievements associated with the counsels of arrangement, the contracts of appointment, and the commands of assignment. He is the First as the Conciliator in mediation, the Covenant in salvation, the Commissioner in evangelization, and the Compensator in remuneration. Nothing comparable to this comprehensive claim, condensed to the compass of a single verse, is to be found elsewhere in all literature. The boundless regions with their manifold dimensions of dignity and dominion, and the endless duration of our Lord's durability and distinction are altogether overwhelming. The very nature of the declaration, ranging as it does from bygone ages on to the far-flung regions of eternal destiny, is certainly far too profound to be the invention of imagination and is certainly far beyond the bounds of human investigation to explore.

Between these terminal points to which Christ refers lie all His prerogatives of might and majesty in leadership and lord-ship, all His potentialities of ability and authority in headship, and heirship, and all His principalities in spiritual dominion and devotion in messiahship and mediatorship. Such words as these, "I am the first and the last," befit no other lips but His, and belong to no other being save the one Mediator between God and men, the man Christ Jesus (1 Tim. 2:5). He it is who mediated for Adam, Abel, and Abraham. He held this office before the world began, and in His omniscient understanding of all things He knows of no successor. The function fulfilled by Aaron on earth was but a miniature figure of the true. From His primordial standing in His pristine High Priesthood as the First, to the perfecting of His purchased possession in prevailing ministry as the Last, Christ appears, and acquires the riches of the glory of His inheritance in the saints, everyone of whom is to be conformed to His image, with bodies fash-ioned like to His body.

We cannot contemplate any issues greater than these, or any goal more grandly impressive. Christ in His mastery prevails perfectly, triumphs thoroughly, conquers completely, and fulfills finally and forever the entire mandate of Deity, in order to establish Light, Life, and Love in a lasting heritage, which is incorruptible, undefiled, and that fadeth not away.

THE I AM OF INCOMPREHENSIBILITY

I am the root and offspring of David, and the bright and morning star (Rev. 22:16).

A root is very obscure and covered up, whereas a star is most obvious and conspicuous. Many features about the life of Christ are mysterious and concealed from view, while the ma-jority are manifest and reveal His virtue. Christ as the Root preceded David and produced his life, decreed his anointing, designated his name, determined his dominion, directed the development of his generous disposition, delegated his authority, delivered him from his enemies, disclosed to him the pattern of the temple, disciplined his character, and demanded a whole-hearted observance of His divine law. As the offspring of David, Christ appeared in a special family line which is termed "the house of David" (Luke 1:69); in a stated birthplace, "the city of David" (Luke 2:4); with a sovereign right of claim, the throne of David (Luke (1:32); with the secret of kingly power, "the key of David" (Rev. 3:7), and a score of other relative features.

"I am the God of Abraham" expresses much in connection with the patriarch, but "I am the root of David" explains much more in relation to the prince of Israel. In relation to the first, Christ said, "God is not the God of the dead, but of the living"; so Abraham lives. Likewise also, "I am the root of David" imples that this root never dies; so then David ever lives in life everlasting.

What a sensational part Christ has played throughout all the centuries in the lives of outstanding characters of Bible history. He is the God of Abraham, the Fear of Isaac (Gen. 31:42), the King of Jacob, the Blesser of Joseph, the Lion of Judah, the Sword of Gideon, the Rod of Jesse, the Root of David, the Hope of Israel, and suchlike, capacities in which no one but He could possibly function. The seven greatest victories in the life of David the beloved were gained single-handedly; likewise the seven grandest conquests in the life of Christ the beloved were secured alone. In the twelve great capacities in the life of David—servant and sovereign, shepherd and steward, singer and soldier, and suchlike—Christ by far exceeded him in each and every feature.

But the link Christ had with humanity and humility was by an act of His own volition. He voluntarily took on Himself the form of a servant and was found in fashion as a man and humbled Himself (Phil. 2:7). "I am the bright, the morning star" directs our attention to His underived splendor associated with His undelegated grandeur in heavenly glory; a glory which He had with the Father before the world was.

"Though He was rich, yet for your sakes He became poor" (2 Cor. 8:9). When was Christ rich? He it was who brought celestial relations into the terrestrial realm and descended from His lofty lordship to a lowly lineage. Seeing that He has such a background, we are not surprised to hear Him ask the Pharisees the question, "What think ye of Christ? whose son is He? They say unto Him, The son of David. He said unto them, How then doth David in spirit call Him Lord, saying, The Lord said unto my Lord, Sit thou on My right hand, till I make Thine enemies Thy footstool? If David then call Him Lord, how is He his son? And no man was able to answer Him a word" (Matt. 22:42-45).

On the occasion recorded, the royalists were present, those who devoted their loyalty to king Herod. The rationalists were there, they who denied a life hereafter. The ritualists also interrogated Him, a community that had devised a traditional system of their own. But none could refute the wisdom of His replies, for the I AM is the omniscient one.

In this final message when Christ makes use of the I AM title for the last time in Scripture and unites it with the root and offspring of David, and star of the morning, He impresses His divine insignia on the Word of God as being an organic whole. His declaration verifies the unity of prophetical truth, the authenticity of Biblical records, the harmony of doctrinal teaching, and the inviolability of spiritual revelation.

"The morning star" is the last symbolical statement Christ makes use of in His communication to John on Patmos concerning the divine character of His supreme sovereignty and supernatural splendor. It is a marvelous highlight in the interpreting of the mysterious powers He wielded and the matchless predictions He made during His earthly ministry. An ageless maturity is signified by this figure.

The star is a magnificent symbol of sovereignty in the widest sense of administration. Christ is starlike in both His generous sufficiency and glorious superiority, and continues His course undeflected in procedure and undiverted in purpose. The star is a monumental sign of authority, and is so depicted in Numbers 24:17. The star of empire is used at coronations in Britain and as the insignia of high-ranking officers in the armies of the United States. Christ holds the seven stars in His right hand in the opening chapter of this unveiling, in demonstration of His absolute ability to rule righteously and resolutely. The star is a majestic seal of constancy, for there is no variableness or shadow of turning in this category, and we know our Lord and Saviour never varies in vitality or virtue, but is the same yesterday, today, and forever.

Many other marks of majesty are attached to this sensational claim but we must content ourselves by saying that the bright, the morning star, in reference to the Saviour, portrays a splendid picture of His complete authority, copious ministry, competent ability, continuous sufficiency, coronated majesty, and captivating beauty. He is well qualified to usher in the cloudless dawn of a deathless dominion in His everlasting kingdom, to whom be glory forever and ever.

One day the clock of time shall verge to its last hour, the hoary pillars of earth will crumble, the age-old monoliths and mansions tumble, world dynasties shall once for all disappear, the mountains and the hills depart in final upheaval, the fields of battle, fertilized by the blood of the slain, shall give up their dead, the sea shall give up the millions engulfed in its ocean main, the elements shall melt with fervent heat, and "the Lord alone shall be exalted in that day" (Is. 2:17). Our richest hopes rise in rhythm to rapturous heights at the radiant prospect of His return. He never retracts a promise, He never relinquishes His power, He never repeals His pledge. "Behold, I come quickly; and My reward is with Me, to give every man according as his work shall be" (Rev. 22:12).

In these three groups where this astounding title or amazing Name is used, we are introduced initially and instructively, to the *identity* of the *person*, implicitly and illuminatively to the *intimacy* of His *presence*, and ideally and illustriously to the *infinity* of His *power*. His Name stands in priority to all, and He is Finality. "For of Him, and through Him, and to Him, are all things: to whom be glory forever. Amen" (Rom. 11:36).

J

The most famous and fascinating name known to mankind, more familiar in its meaning and much more fragrant to memory than that of any other character.

JESUS (Matt. 1:21)
> Full of charm and comfort.

JESUS CHRIST (Heb. 13:9)
> Free from change and compromise.

JESUS IS THE CHRIST, THE SON OF GOD (John 20:31)
> Foremost in rank and renown.

JESUS CHRIST THE LORD (Rom. 7:24-25)
> First in authority and administration.

THE JUSTIFIER (Rom. 3:26)
> Famous in erasing evidences of guilt.

THE JUDGE (Gen. 18:25)
> Final in justice and judgment.

THE JASPER STONE (Rev. 4:2-3)
> Fascinating in beauty and purity.

THE JUST ONE (Acts 7:52)
> Faultless in fidelity and faithfulness.

A JEW (John 4:9)
> Fraternal in friendship and fellowship.

JESUS THE KING (Matt. 26:36)
> Fairest in regality and righteousness.

JEHOVAH OF HOSTS (Is. 44:6)
> Fullness in greatness and graciousness.

JAH (Ps. 68:4)
> Formidable in strength and supremacy.

HIS NAME SHALL BE CALLED JESUS

Jesus is the Bright Name full of the light of life.
Jesus is the Sweet Name full of the perfume of praise.
Jesus is the Heart Name full of the music of love.
Jesus is the Rest Name full of the purpose of peace.
Jesus is the Best Name full of the treasure of truth.
Jesus is the Great Name full of the wealth of wisdom.
Jesus is the Gift Name full of the grace of God.

THAT IN THE NAME OF JESUS EVERY KNEE SHOULD BOW

Thy name our hearts and minds adore,
   In Thee we find our treasure store,
None other can Thy grace outvie,
   Coming to save and justify.

Thy name the refuge of the heart,
   No power can bid us thence depart,
Thy merit reaches to the sky,
   Thy hand hath power to justify.

Thou art our Life, our Light, our All,
   No dread of death can now appall,
Thy name alone can satisfy,
   For Thou hast died to justify.

Glad hope that hovers o'er the soul,
   Engraven on a mighty scroll,
Thy Word, that bids the dead arise,
   Proclaims the truth that justifies.

Like sweet perfumes Thy names ascend,
   Thy praise and fame are without end,
The hosts above forever cry,
   He died! He rose! to justify!

Thy names throughout the years unfold
Like precious gems and burnished gold.
One priceless treasure faith espies
That blessed name that justifies.

C. J. R.

I am Alpha and Omega (Rev. 22:13)

The precious personality of Jesus the Saviour stands out in history as more distinguished than any other dignitary, more prominent than any other potentate, more conspicuous than any other celebrity, and more appealing than any other authority. He exceeds in His kingly merit all other monarchs in majesty and excels all other governors in greatness and glory. His name is more widely known than any other worthy, and His many titles are printed annually, millions of times more than the combined number of the twelve most notable characters of history. The spiritual values of His unsearchable riches of grace and goodness, and the spacious vastness of His inscrutable resources are altogether beyond the range of human reckoning. Jesus is more desired and more despised than anyone else. His life and ministry receive more commendation and more condemnation than those of anyone in the universe. The most outstanding record that is graven on the scroll of time is the date of His birth, and no issued document is legal, no signed check is valid, and no business receipt is of value unless it bears the statistical reference to this great historic event. The fame of His name lives on with ever-increasing renown. The memory of His loving-kindness is undying in its attractive charm. The ministry of His graciousness is unforgettable in its thoughtful considerateness. The mercy of His goodness which so reflects His divine nature is wholly unlike that of any other patriot. The mastery of His meekness which harnessed His infinite might to minister to man's needs is one of the unending marvels of the ages. The majesty of His kingliness is maintained to this hour, unchallenged by any other claimant. The mystery of His Godlikeness as described by Paul the apostle is undeniable, for no one else has fully demonstrated a complete obedience to the divine will in all things as Christ did.

The life of Jesus evinces throughout the everlastingness of the spirit of youthfulness, for in doing the will of God He abides forever. He expressed a vitality that never varied, exhibited a virtue that never changed, and enjoyed a vision that never dimmed nor diminished. The radiant life, resplendent light, and redolent love that characterized all His activities were but a faint display of His immortal glories. How is it possible for any finite being to interpret His infinite character which is so perfectly complete and permanently constant? Jesus of Nazareth set forth His credentials in self-abnegating service, He sealed His claims by supreme sacrifice, He shielded His character by serene silence, He showed forth His compassion by submissive suffering, He selected His companions by sacerdotal supplication, and He secured His conquest as an all- sufficient Saviour by substitution.

If we contemplate the characteristics of His constancy, focus our faith on the faithfulness of His fidelity, and spend considerable time concentrating on the generosity of His gracious gift, we shall find good reason for loving Him with all our heart and mind and strength. Let us remember that He is greater than all He bestows, better than all His blessings, and lovelier than all the gifts He lavishes on His loved ones. His pervading personality dominated the history, prophecy, and verity of revealed truth. At this stage we arrive at some of the best known names and titles of our beloved Saviour which begin with the letter J.

JESUS

> Thou shalt call His name JESUS: for He shall save His people from their sins (Matt. 1:21).

The Hebrew equivalent of this name is *Joshua*, which means, "Jehovah the Saviour," or, "Jehovah will save." The Greek designation means virtually the same, together with the additional insight into its inner significance as declared by the prophet, which signifies that it includes in its meaning, "God with us." The references in which *Joshua* is rendered *Jesus* are found in Acts 7:4-5 and Hebrews 4:8. How suggestive that the Old Testament word is appended to a prince, a prophet, and a priest. Jesus in the New Testament is all three. As a name, *Jesus* is more grandly honored and more grievously hated, more acclaimed and more accused than any other. We find it imprinted over six hundred times on the pages of the four Gospels, and it is the most charming, consoling, comforting name by which our beloved Saviour is known. We are aware that all the sweetest hymns, the richest poems, and choicest music are woven about its wealth of value and worth of virtue.

The name stands as a synonym for free healing, friendly help, and full salvation, and is broadcast today in a thousand languages. Jesus was the first in this world to be called the Friend of sinners. As a title, the name signifies that Jesus is the veracity of truth, the visibility of God, the verity of love, and the victory of grace in all perfection. From heavenly altitudes He descended to the level of humanity, and transformed temporal things with His tender touch, while His teaching of celestial truth transfigured the lives of men.

Enshrined in this precious title are the richest theme in music, the sweetest note in song, the worthiest word in worship, and the princeliest name in praise. The One who bears this designation of delightful dignity is the fairest Flower in the fragrant garden of virtue, the rarest Treasure in the palatial mansion of truth, the greatest Gift amid the riches of eternal glory, the loveliest Legacy in the lasting heritage of life, the brightest Ray in the brilliant beams of ineffable light, the purest Pleasure in the peerless delights of perennial peace, and the choicest Companion in the celestial courts of communal love. How we revel in the glories of His wondrous grace, while we devotedly sing in worshipful praise.

> Jesus, the very thought of Thee
> With sweetness fills my breast;
> But sweeter far Thy face to see,
> And in Thy presence rest.

Jesus, the name that charms our fears,
That bids our sorrows cease;
'Tis music in the sinners' ears;
'Tis life and health and peace.

* * *

Jesus shall reign where'er the sun
Doth his successive journeys run;
His kingdom stretch from shore to shore,
Till moons shall wax and wane no more.

* * *

Jesus is the sweetest name I know,
And He's just the same as His lovely name.
And that's the reason why I love Him so,
For Jesus is the sweetest name I know.

* * *

Come, let us sing the matchless worth
Of Him who came in lowly birth,
And died to save our ruined race,
Jesus, the blessed Lord of grace.

* * *

To Jesus every day I find my heart is closer drawn,
He's fairer than the glory of the gold and purple dawn,
He's all my fancy pictured in its fairest dreams and more,
Each day He grows still sweeter than He was the day before.

The eternal Father meant this name to mean more than any other. That is why He bestowed it upon His beloved Son. If we carefully consider its fullness of meaning, we shall find it to be the best and most suited that could possibly be borne by One who was sent to save from sin. For it is very evident that the sick of soul needed healing, the far and faulty needed redeeming, the bad and banished needed reconciling, the cruel and corrupt needed regenerating, and the lost and lone needed saving. The Saviour is the only One who can adequately meet these various needs. Paul presents the case negatively and says, "Know ye not that the unrighteous shall not inherit the kingdom of God? Be not deceived: neither fornicators, nor idolaters, nor adulterers, nor effeminate, nor abusers of themselves with mankind, nor thieves, nor covetous, nor drunkards, nor revilers, nor extortioners, shall inherit the kingdom of God. And such were some of you: But ye are washed, but ye are sanctified, but ye are justified in the name of the Lord Jesus, and by the Spirit of our God" (1 Cor. 6:9-11). These ten classes have been appropriately referred to as the ten lepers. How grandly the title *Jesus* befits the One who can grapple with such deplorable cases and not only deliver, but save to the uttermost and perfect forever them that are set apart.

Therefore, this blessed name is like honey to the taste, harmony to the ear, health to the soul and hope to the heart. When we attempt to tabulate the treasure, with the weight of wealth, the value of virtue, the measure of merit, and to estimate the excellence, price the perfection, and calculate the comfort contained in His name, we are astounded at the riches of grace and riches of glory that therein reside. Is not the name *Jesus* a pearl from paradise and a gem from the gloryland? Is it not a sapphire from the heavenly sanctuary of the Most High?

Yea, it causes the enlargement before our minds of God's mine of mercy, and enriches greatly His legacy of love. To an undefinable degree, the name enhances the harp of hope, engraces the jewels of joy, embellishes the vessels of virtue, endears the mansions of memories, and ennobles the sweetest of songs. Jesus still stands loftiest in renown, He soars highest in rank and sits chiefest in rule, governing in the power of an endless life, enthroned a Priest forever.

> Jesus! Name of all names above, Jesus best and nearest,
> Jesus! Fount of perfect love, Holiest, tenderest, dearest,
> Jesus! Source of grace repletest, Jesus choicest, sweetest,
> Jesus! Saviour all divine, Thy name forever, only Thine.

JESUS CHRIST

> Jesus Christ, the same yesterday, and today, and forever (Heb. 13:8).

The character of Jesus Christ as presented in the Epistle to the Hebrews overshadows and outshines all the worthies of bygone history, and outclasses and outvies the prophets, priests, and kings of the Old Testament economy.

Twelve of the institutional, inspirational, and instructional systems are specifically referred to as having been surpassed, consisting of the prophetic, the angelic, the Adamic, the Abrahamic, the Mosaic, the Sabbatic, the post-Exilic, the Davidic, the Aaronic, the symbolic, the ritualistic, and the historic. Concerning this last one, we are aware that no conspicuous event ever transpires without an outstanding character. Wherefore, in chapter 11 we are introduced to twenty-one distinguished leaders who were witnesses, workers, warriors, and worshipers, in all of whose lives Jesus is the Author of their venture of faith, their vision of hope, and their virtue of love (see 12:2). With all the expenditure of these values through the years, in the promotion of character suitable to dwell in the eternal city, there has been no diminution or depletion of His wisdom and power, for "Jesus Christ [is] the same yesterday, and today, and forever."

The name Jesus is faith's strongest rock, hope's brightest star, and love's holiest shrine. The One who bears it has entranced poets and enhanced their words, enraptured musicians and enriched their harmonies, enthralled artists and enlarged their visions, and has enlightened scholars and enlivened their research.

Jesus is truth's fairest Jewel, time's choicest Theme, life's strongest Cord, light's clearest Ray, purity's whitest Peak, joy's deepest Tide, and glory's stateliest Summit. Very few subjects in this world remain fresh enough and attractive enough to provoke continual attention and to draw out sustained admiration; but in Jesus Christ we realize a personal Character from whose attractive charm new lights and perfections flow ceaselessly, and from whom fresh beauties and by whom free bounties are continually furnished. His riches are unsearchable, His virtues inestimable, and His glories indescribable. Jesus Christ is always Himself, the same forever. His memorable attributes are exhibited in His mediatorial atonement, while His majestic abilities are expressed in His ministerial achievement, demonstrating the principles of the kingdom of God and defeating the powers of the kingdom of darkness.

The vessels of the sanctuary of the tabernacle of old signify the values of His virtuous character. Four of these were made of pure gold. The preciousness of the golden mercy seat above the ark, with its glittering crown and glistening cherubim, assured His royal pardon. The redolent perfume of the golden incense altar, designed to diffuse its rich fragrance throughout the sacred sanctuary, told of the sweet savor of the Saviour's sacrifice for our acceptance. The priceless values of the gorgeous lampstand resembled the light of His divine glory, who holds the seven stars in His right hand. The priestly sustenance of the golden shewbread table, with its suggestive symbolism of satisfying grace, revealed the sufficiency of supply for spiritual life in Him who is the Bread of God sent down from Heaven. Yet all of these combined fail to show the measure of His wealth and worthiness. They were revealed to contribute in part to our understanding of the fame and fullness wrapped up in His wonderful name.

This blessed One, the Beloved of the Father, is the Captain of our faith, the Guardian of our hope, the Custodian of our love, the Bastion of our strength, the Champion of our right, the Meridian of our light, and the Escutcheon of our life (Col. 3:3). We would fain place references to each of these, but space forbids.

We find the title, *Jesus Christ the Chosen of God*, engraven on the entire record of the New Testament. Standing highest in renown, sounding loudest in acclaim, shining brightest in esteem, and echoing sweetest in refrain is this heaven-born name Jesus. View Him from whatever angle we will, He is altogether lovely. What rare melody resounds from His ministry, what rich mercy rebounds from His mediation, and what royal majesty reflects from His messiahship. We are commanded in the Epistle to the Hebrews to consider Him who endured such contradiction of sinners against Himself; and if we do, we can but be arrested and amazed at the fervor of His zeal, the manner of His work, the ardor of His love, the valor of His courage, the splendor of His power, the grandeur of His grace, and the honor of His name.

Mary of Bethany believed Him to be worthy of the best she could bestow, and brought to Him her alabaster box of very costly spikenard. The rich perfume distilled from a thousand blooms grown in a league of rose gardens was not too precious for her to lavish upon Him. Jesus, our blessed Lord, is deserving of far more than our gratitude for blessings received; we should give generously of our love which well befits His deserts from us.

Let us honor Him highly with the homage of our hearts, worship Him worthily with mind and strength, praise Him persistently for His essential resource as a Redeemer, for His established right to redeem, and most of all for His earnest resolve to pay the ransom for our redemption in His own blood, without which His merit and majesty would have availed us nought.

> O how sweet the glorious message simple faith may claim;
> Yesterday, today, forever, Jesus is the same.
> Still He loves to save the sinful, heal the sick and lame,
> Cheer the mourner, still the tempest, glory to His name.
>
> A. B. SIMPSON

JESUS IS THE CHRIST, THE SON OF GOD

Many other signs truly did Jesus in the presence of His disciples which are not written in this book, but these are written that ye might believe that Jesus is the Christ, the Son of God (John 20:31).

This statement centers the underlying hopes of undying aspirations of the Hebrew people and focuses them on the Person whom John identifies as Jesus the Christ, the Son of God. We are told in the book of the Acts of the Apostles that Jesus was approved of God, which confirms that His words, His works, and His ways were a verification of His identity. The approval given in Mark's Gospel is threefold.

The voice from Heaven said, "This is My beloved Son, in whom I am well pleased." Whose image and superscription is this? Why, the Father's. But a worthy witness preceded the heavenly testimony in the voice of the herald from the wilderness. Later there followed a third testimony, the voice of one demon-possessed (Mark 1:3,11,24-26). So His character is certified by Heaven, by humanity, and by hell.

In this triple title, the echoes of the eternal and obscure blend with the temporal and obvious in the person of the beloved Son. *Jesus,* the name linked with atoning sacrifice, is coupled with *Christ,* a title which means "the anointed of God." The terrestrial activity and celestial authority are pictured operating in spiritual harmony in the Son. This accounts for the degree of mystery associated with His manifestation, the divine mercy attendant upon His mediation, and the delightful memory attached to His ministration.

We should be deeply moved as we listen to the divine declaration of distinction made by the eternal Father when He broke the silence of heavenly stillness, by saying, "This is My beloved Son." A clear prediction had been given centuries before that Jehovah would declare such a decree (Ps. 2:7), to which is added the words, "this day have I begotten Thee." This statement is not made with reference to the beginning of personal existence or being, but with reference to an initiation to a work, ministry, or purpose. The matter is of similar character as to that of Christ's being brought into manifest sonship by the resurrection, which fact is declared by the Spirit of holiness (Rom. 1:3-4).

If Jesus is only an unusually upright man and nothing more, He cannot be a final authority for mankind in lordship, headship, heirship, and judgeship. But He is much more than an exemplary man; "[He is] the Christ, the Son of the living God." This assures us that He is in full identity of being with

Deity. As Jesus, He is the Truth and Testator for redemption; as Christ, He is the Test and Touchstone of our relationship with Heaven; as Son of God, He expresses true likeness of will and the same transcendent loveliness with the Father. Wherefore, man may find in Jesus a Redeemer, in Christ a Reconciler, and in the Son a Regenerator. Other writers have pointed out that there are two different words used for Son in Psalm 2. The first is rendered *Ben* as in *Benjamin;* the second is rendered *Bar,* as in *Barabbas.* Each of these means identity of personality, but they also contain a difference. *Ben,* Son, as in verse 7, indicates that which Christ achieves. As Firstborn He builds God's spiritual house. *Bar,* in verse 12, suggests that which He receives as Heir. The one relates to His honor, the other to His heritage; the former to His lordship, the latter to His legacy.

We miss a great deal in relation to Pilate's offer to the nation in the matter of a choice, if we fail to notice that the name of the murderer Bar-abbas means "Son of the father," and that Christ had twice been attested Son of the Father (Mark 1:11; 9:7). The malefactor was the expression of vice and violence, the Messiah the exhibition of verity and virtue. "Alas for public impulse, the Lord is crucified; it clamoured for Barabbas, and God's own Son denied" (Haldane). The tragic result has been that this sad world has been ravaged by vice and violence ever since.

We should notice particularly that Christ is declared to be the Son of God from the very first verse of Mark's Gospel, and the title *son,* occurs twenty-eight times in the message. Therefore, in the light of the Father's inscription from above, He has a perfect right and title to the inheritance, a fact recorded in Psalm 2. "This is the heir; come, let us kill him, and the inheritance shall be ours," we are given an insight into the full meaning of His mission (Mark 12:7).

Christ bore and wore the credentials of His noble office not in gold encinctured decorations that glitter and perish, but in the great and gracious discharge of His legal and moral obligations as Heir, and by His payment of ransom to redeem the estate through one supreme sacrifice. The merit and memorial of these ministries are immortal.

The mention of the right hand six times in Mark's Gospel throws a flood of light on Christ's heirship and headship (see, for example, 12:7-8,35-36; also 14:62; 16:19). In the last of these references the Lord is described as the Maintainer of the activities carried on by the disciples, as they seek to secure the distant outposts of the territory belonging to the rightful heir. If we may be permitted a suggestion concerning one of the prominent values in each of the three titles of our heading, we would say:

As Jesus, He is the Buyer, who pays the ransom for salvation and sanctification.

As Christ, He is the Builder, who provides the resource for construction and completion.

As Son, He is the Bestower, who prepares the residence for union and communion.

This eternal home, in an everlasting heritage, is the erstwhile, age-abiding hope of the redeemed of the Lord.

> Take the name of Jesus with you,
> Child of sorrow and of woe;
> It will joy and comfort give you,
> Take it, then, where'er you go.
>
> L. BAXTER

JESUS CHRIST THE LORD

O wretched man that I am! Who shall deliver me from the body of this death? I thank God through Jesus Christ our Lord (Rom. 7:24-25).

In their combination, these three titles express His atoning passion, His anointed person, and His administrative power. John the apostle declares that the main purpose he had in view when writing the gospel message was that we might believe that Jesus is the Christ, that is, the Messiah.

The title *Jesus*, as a name for the Son of God, was predetermined by God's appointment, and the divine selection was first made known to Joseph through Gabriel's announcement

(Matt. 1:20-21). No name was ever attended with greater honor. Chosen and bestowed by high Heaven, it remains as the name of names to this present hour, with all its providential tokens. Verily, His name is also supreme in the home, where we enjoy social benefits; in the house of God, where devout worship is presented in Spirit and in truth; and in Heaven itself, the heritage of the redeemed, where He is acclaimed altogether worthy.

The unusual Person who bears these titles is so inexpressibly lovable and so inconceivably likable that the charm of His character and the cheer of His constancy are alike unutterable. *Jesus* is a joyous name which has awakened more gladness and promoted more rejoicing throughout the whole world than any other. How the redeemed of the Lord revel in singing that beautiful hymn of praise, "Jesus, Thou Joy of Loving Hearts." Yea it is also a famous name, for the Bearer's fame spread abroad during His earthly manifestation and has continued to increase to this very day. "True image of the infinite, whose essence is concealed: brightness of uncreated light, the heart of God revealed" (Josiah Conder). Furthermore, to Him belongs a precious name that can never be equaled or excelled. All precious is Jesus, our Master and Friend, whose kingdom and riches abide without end. The throne of His grace is established and sure, the fame of His name shall forever endure. But He has a gracious name, for of His fullness have all we received and grace for grace. He is gracious toward all in a most graceful manner. Yes, and *Jesus* is a wondrous name. On seven occasions in Luke's Gospel He awakened wonder by what He said and did. Much more so is His name lustrous and glorious because of triumphs gained and by virtue of His transforming grace, overcoming all manner of trials and in overthrowing all foes of the human soul.

The suitable fitness and sustained fullness of Jesus in His rare qualifications to administer every position of power and sway every scepter of sovereignty and to hold every high and honorable office is a subject imprinted on the entire scope of the New Testament. Such titles as, *King, Lord, Ruler, Governor, Shepherd, Saviour, Firstborn,* and *Forerunner* are all attached to it. The mystery of His deity which is linked with His manifest humanity is an unfathomable wonder. Wherefore the triple title, *Jesus Christ the Lord,* combines the stateliest features of earthly and heavenly nature of personality to express His supreme lordship.

This ideal of one central complete control of all administrative power approaches the very crux of the real secret of all things. Amos the prophet, when contrasting this vital authority with the vanities of idolatry, uses the great title *Lord (Adonahy)* (Amos 5:3) in connection with His rain-making and replete ruling administration, in the exercise of a controlling lordship (5:8). The ancient Greeks spoke of the seven stars referred to in Amos as Pleiades, a fact which is linked here with Orion (see also Job 38:31). Modern astronomy affirms that this mighty constellation of Pleiades is the central governing force of the entire universe. How very suggestive therefore that Jesus the Lord should be revealed holding the seven stars in His right hand, a significant sign of what He claimed before He ascended: "All power is given to Me, in heaven and in earth."

No realm of authority or ruling ability in administration exists where this does not apply. Jesus as Lord holds every form of power within the orbit of His omnipotent might. Therefore, Jesus is Lord of love and legislation, the two fundamental principles of a lasting kingdom. Jesus as Lord is the Regenerator and Reconciler, without whom there is no spiritual life and stable liberty. Jesus as Lord is the Author of eternal salvation and satisfaction; apart from Him there could be no true sanctity and security. Jesus as Lord supervises service and sacrifice, assuring hope and holiness, pleasure and permanence (Ps. 16:11). This same applies to every feature and factor of the fullness of Godhead which resides in Him bodily. Therefore, if we desire life we must not reject Him, if we need light we must not refuse Him, if we crave love we must not neglect Him, if we pursue joy we must not omit Him, if we want peace we must not exclude Him, if we demand truth we must not ignore Him, if we need power we must not forsake Him, if we long for rest we must not turn away from Him, because Jesus the Lord is all and in all. The word *all* in this verse is used in the plural both times, which implies, Christ is all of every spiritual benefit and blessing everywhere, eternally. The abundances assured in the atonement are amplified in the almighty One, "For in Him dwelleth all the fulness of the Godhead bodily. And ye are complete [or filled up] in Him, which is the head of all principality and power" (Col. 2:9-10).

> Fairest Lord Jesus, Ruler of all nature,
> O Thou of God and man the Son,
> Thee will I cherish, Thee will I honor,
> Thou my soul's glory, joy, and crown.
> *Crusaders' Hymn*

THE JUSTIFIER

To declare . . . at this time His righteousness: that He might be just, and the justifier of him which believeth in Jesus (Rom. 3:26).

By Him all that believe are justified from all things, from which ye could not be justified by the law of Moses (Acts 13:39).

Among the many spiritual blessings of the gospel, this stands out as one of the most cheerful and consoling, for it gives us the greatest guarantee of complete clearance from the guilt of sin, together with the entire erasure of every trace of evidence of former guiltiness, so that no charge can ever be laid against us forever, for the case can never be reopened. Who shall lay anything to the charge of God's elect? Where is there anyone anywhere in existence who can condemn me? The omniscient God who fully knows everything has justified me. The secret of this knowledge and how to obtain it was one of Job's eight crucial questions. "How can a man be just with God?" Apart from the wisdom of God, the provision of God, the option of God, the sanction of God, and the action of God, justification could never exist, for the motive, the means, and the medium of securing justification are entirely from God.

We may gain a clearer understanding of the marvel of it, if

we glance at four of the phases in which the matter is presented in the New Covenant, and this should also give us a deeper appreciation of our marvelous Justifier. The judicial phrase of justification is related to Godhead: "God that justifieth" (Rom. 8:33). The court is set, the charge is laid and the culprit is condemned to death. The defense answers, "It is Christ that died." The accusing council immediately says, All men die; the fact that Christ died is no criterion. The defense answers, "Who is risen again." To this the objection is raised, What proof does that supply that God accepts the substitute? The defense answers, "Who is even at the right hand of God." So God did accept the sacrifice. Then the objection is offered, The prisoner is well aware that since he claimed to believe that Christ died, rose, and ascended to the right hand of God on his behalf, his life has not been faultless, stainless, and sinless; therefore the condemnation stands. The defense answers, "Who continually maketh intercession for us." That intercession, according to Hebrews, saves to the uttermost (Heb. 7:25). Wherefore, in the presence of God's holiness I am judicially justified.

The mediatorial phase of justification stands in relation to the Christ of God. "A man is not justified by the works of the law, but by the faith of Jesus Christ, even we have believed in Jesus Christ, that we might be justified by the faith of Christ, and not by the works of the law" (Gal. 2:16). Three ways of self-help face the soul: self-preparation, self-reformation, and self-justification. But these are of no account before God's tribunal. Identity with Christ in crucifixion is the only solution to my problem (Gal. 2:20). The law provides no constraining principle and no contributing power to encourage glad obedience and good behavior. Christ crucified, raised, and ascended contributes both. Obedience to God, love to Christ, and joy in the Holy Spirit are not prompted and promoted by the law, but by justifying grace. Salvation by grace ever provokes good works, but salvation by good works never promotes grace. Christ the qualified Advocate, knowing full well my accountability, appeared for me before the heavenly tribunal, acknowledged my guilt, answered the claims of divine justice, and atoned for all grievances against me, so that I am not only completely cleared, but clothed with the comeliness of the sinless One. The opinion of the theologian or logician matters not, seeing that the sole Justifier Himself assures me of justification.

> He made the myriad stars to shine,
> He set the ocean's boundary line;
> To all who on His Word rely,
> He wields the power to justify.

> C. J. R.

The sacrificial aspect of justification contributes another reason for confidence: "Much more then, being now justified by His blood, we shall be saved from wrath through Him" (Rom. 5:9). Our personal merit and good behavior did not secure this benefit, for the previous verse declares that while we were yet sinners Christ died for us. Not what I do, but what He did, justifies. His atoning blood ratifies the fact that my sin is remitted, so I may rest assured that all charges have been removed and that I am ready to receive as a gift the robe of God's righteousness. Having been accused, I am now acquitted, all offenses are obliterated, accusations are abolished, every evidence of wrongdoing has been effaced, the case can never be reopened, the Judge calls for the court to be dismissed.

> Bold shall I stand in the great day,
> For who aught to my charge shall lay?

The legal and moral aspects of justification supply further confirmation for us to revel in. "Being justified freely by His grace through the redemption that is in Christ Jesus. . . . To declare . . . at this time His righteousness: that He might be just, and the justifier of him which believeth in Jesus" (Rom. 3:24,26). The word *law* is used seventy-seven times in this Epistle, and every feature of salvation is presented as being legally and morally sound. Not only has the moral law been upheld but justice has been honored, righteousness has been magnified, and God glorified. No flaw or fault can be found in the method and means God has adopted to achieve His purpose of justifying the ungodly. In His integrity He remains perfectly just; not a single detail of the righteous nature of His throne has been surrendered. The divine attributes glow with new luster at Golgotha, the radiance of righteousness was never brighter, the triumph of truth was never greater, the splendor of love was never stronger, the honor of holiness was never upheld to such a degree of worthiness, as in the Cross of Christ. "They found no cause of death in Him . . . by Him all that believe are justified from all things, from which ye could not be justified by the law of Moses" (Acts 13:28,39).

What better illustration could we have of justification than Peter's own case? He slept when he should have watched with Christ in Gethsemane. When awakened by the rabble crowd, he drew his sword and lunged forward to strike the nearest assailant. Malchus evidently dodged the blow, but lost his ear. Later, in the palace of the high priest, Peter was accused and denied the accusation. Why did the accusers not bring Malchus the servant of the high priest forward as evidence of what Peter had done? They dare not; Christ had restored the ear, and there was no scar. Peter had been justified and could not be convicted. He had no cause to deny Christ, for the Saviour had already shielded and secured him from the penalty of Roman law. No human agency or authority could lift man from his state of guilt, transform his character, advance him to noble rank, and cause him to stand in a position in which he is unassailable by law, unchallengeable by justice, and unaccusable by evidence. Jesus only is the Justifier.

> Jesus our Lord, with what joy we adore Thee,
> Chanting our praise to Thyself on the throne!
> Blest in Thy presence we worship before Thee,
> Own Thou art worthy, and worthy alone.

H. D'A. CHAMPNEY

THE JUDGE

Shall not the Judge of all the earth do right? (Gen. 18:25)
The Father judgeth no man, but hath committed all judg-
ment unto the Son (John 5:22).
As I hear, I judge: and My judgment is just (John 5:30).
If I judge, My judgment is true: for I am not alone, but I and
the Father that sent Me (John 8:16).
God the Judge of all (Heb. 12:23).

In all final and faithful judicial proceedings, Christ Jesus is
the Chief Justice. The demonstrations He has already given to
mankind justify the justice of His judgeship. One whole book
in the Old Testament is devoted to a record of the days when
the Judges ruled in Israel. The justice administered in Ruth's
case, at the gate of Bethlehem, was given during this period
(Ruth 1:1; 4:1). The tribunal at the gate of the city is a feature
in the Scriptures that runs from Genesis to Malachi. Even in
the city of Jerusalem, the gate Miphkad was appointed for this
purpose. In the light of the ability and disability of the many
personages discharging this great and important function, it is
most refreshing and revealing to meet with One filling this
high office who is perfect in judgeship. The main official duty
required of a judge is to act discreetly, wisely, and justly in all
decisions made. In such matters Jesus Christ stands without a
peer or superior. He alone has the supreme qualifications that
fit a judge to administer justice perfectly. Firstly, in regard to
knowledge, He is omniscient, knowing all the facts about
everyone, everywhere (John 2:25). Secondly, He is omnipotent
and can do anything for anyone, anywhere. Thirdly, He is omnipresent, and is therefore available and accessible to
whosoever will, whensoever the need arises, wheresoever they
may be, with whatsoever kind of case. This Judge is all wise
and almighty, all merciful and all gracious, and no one can
ultimately elude His tribunal, evade His justice, or eschew His
judgment (John 5:28-29; Rev. 20:12). He is not hampered or
handicapped by any of the limitations that baffle human
judges. His intelligence is infinite, and He requires no depart-
mental bureau to investigate a single case, to gain information

as to what occurred, or to when and where it happened. He is wholly impartial and cares not for the status and dignity of anyone. No bribe, or wage of the hand, as it is termed in India, can divert justice from being wrought. He never acts so as to amuse the audience, or to misuse His administration, or to abuse His authority. He exercises the initial and final prerogatives that are essential in judgeship, for He is able to kill and to make alive (Jas. 4:12). He is in sole possession of the character required of a man who issues judgment concerning the faults and failures of others. He stated the terms in the temple court when a delicate case was thrust before him for decision: "He that is without sin among you, let him first cast a stone at her" (John 8:7). He may have cast the first, being sinless, but He did not; so no one else dared.

Throughout the empire of Great Britain, when a judge is functioning in the halls of justice, he wears a wavy, white wig, as a symbol of purity of mind, maturity of wisdom, and finality of decision. Prior to the adoption of this practice in the law courts of England, the Lord Jesus Christ was unveiled in the book of the Revelation, and He is described as having his head and hair white like wool, as white as snow. This does signify in His case purity of mind, for all His thoughts are honest and honorable; and maturity of wisdom, for He is the ancient of days, ageless, timeless, weariless, the One who preceded creation (Prov. 8:22). Yea, and His decisions are final, and beyond His verdict there is no other court of appeal. These capacities of His are combined in the unveiling with His penetrating vision, which is as a flame of fire; with His powerful voice, which is as the sound of many waters; and with His precious virtue, which is girt about the breasts with a golden girdle. As Arbiter, Advocate, and Avenger, there is none like Him; no, nor ever shall be. In His appraisements when judging worthiness or wickedness, He is equally capable of awarding things creditable and of avenging things criminal. As Judge, Christ Jesus abides forever just. His faithfulness is perpetual, for this attribute constitutes the very character of His divine nature. His friendliness is proverbial, for as stated earlier, He was the first in this world to be called the Friend of sinners. His fault-

lessness is perpetual: He contracted no smear or stain although
he contacted the worst of the defiled and lepers. Instead of His
becoming polluted by touching those who were unclean, He
imparted His own purity and remained unspotted by the
world.

What a comingling of credentials is portrayed in the Lord of
life and Judge of all. The authority of His oversight, the accuracy of His insight, the priority of His glory, and the
superiority of His government confirm forever the excellence
of His qualifications as Chief Justice of Heaven's supreme
court. Let us exultingly rejoice because there is One who loved
us and whom we love, sitting at the right hand of God, enthroned in majesty, admired by angels, adored by seraphs, acclaimed by the justified, all of whom ascribe to Him the worship due to His worthiness as the infinite Judge. He is the
glorious Head over all the highest in rank and noblest in dignity. He excels exceedingly, for He rules in nature, reigns in
providence, governs in grace, and judges in righteousness.
What a Ruler! What a Judge!

THE JASPER STONE

> Immediately I was in the spirit: and, behold, a throne was set
> in heaven, and one sat on the throne. And He that sat was to
> look upon like a jasper and a sardine stone: and there was a
> rainbow round about the throne, in sight like unto an emerald
> (Rev. 4:2-3).

Throughout the stately panorama of this book, with its
range of vision and record of victory, no feature is so
fascinating as that of the varied figures and features, in both
signs and symbols, which represent our Lord Jesus Christ. The
Spirit of God, in marshaling the wealth of typology and symbolism revealed in the Old Testament, has harnessed His infinite wisdom in fulfilling His great function to which Christ
referred thrice in John 16:13-15. In order to set forth the
beauties of the sovereign Saviour, the Spirit calls into requisition sun and stars, scrolls and seals, seas and ships, sacred
altars and sharpened sickles, together with scores of other ob-

jects, all of which are made to contribute to the marvelous merits of Messiah, the Prince, in His many vocations. As Son of man, He is described in His prevailing might, consummating the divine purpose, with the seven stars in His hand, the sealed scroll in His hand, the sacred censer in His hand, and the sharp sickle in His hand. These in turn are related to His administrative power in the Church, His executive right in creation, His mediatorial office in the commonwealth of the kingdom, and His adjudicative ability in the cities.

The jasper stone in the present title is the finest form of diamond, of clearest luster. This figure sets forth the durability of our Lord, as well as His desirability. The associations of the scene depicted are those of His covenant-keeping constancy and faithfulness. The rainbow round about the throne recalls the circumstances under which this word covenant was first used in Scripture. To reassure Noah after the flood, the Lord made a covenant with the earth and gave as a token of His perpetual decree the rainbow sign (Gen. 9:13).

The use that is frequently made of precious stones in the Bible is to express the perfections of the divine nature, and this instance is no exception. The nature of Christ is thus represented as crystal clear, in the lambent whiteness of its perfect light, so transparently lovely in exclusive choiceness, and of such beauty in its transcendent luster, for He expresses the very essence of essential pureness. His holy characer is unmarred, unblemished, and unspotted by any taint or stain, or as the Scriptures say, holy, guileless, and undefiled. The merging of His many virtues which harmonize so perfectly and blend so delicately is sufficient warrant for the attracting of our admiration, while the many diadems which bedeck His worthy brow, to betoken His regal conquests in spiritual conflict, deserve our devoutest adoration.

Aside from Jesus Christ the Lord of Glory, where are we to look for a stable foundation in support of moral purity? Where else are we to find a final standard of spiritual piety? Where may we turn for access to the spring of truth and drink at its fountain and secure a lasting satisfaction? Unto you therefore which believe He is the preciousness. This is the very One of whom Peter speaks, the living Stone, elect and precious, foremost in purity of heart, uppermost in fixity of purpose, the uttermost in sincerity of love, and the innermost in transparency of motive, for in each of these excellencies He is without equal. Everything Christ stands for enriches the soul, enlightens the mind, and enlarges the vision. Our highest conceptions of Him are cramped and narrow, our fairest descriptions are dwarfed and paltry, while our grandest statements are shriveled and weak.

Jesus as the Jasper Stone is the Embodiment of all preciousness, the Embellishment of all loveliness, the Ennoblement of all gracefulness, and the Enrichment of all kindliness in one comely personality. No king is so lordly in majesty, no prince is so lofty in dignity, no sovereign is so lowly in humility, and no governor is so lovely in beauty as He. With the manifestation of Messiah all the divine attributes of Deity were made manifest to mankind. He became the Medium of expression for grace, mercy, peace, love, joy, truth, righteousness, goodness, meekness, and every other feature, perfectly. Jesus is the one Jewel of incalculable worth, the costly Gem of indescribable value, the only precious Stone of inestimable price, yea, without price.

The jasper stone is one of the choicest figures of accredited beauty that could possibly be used. How worthily He merits it! His distinguished conquests over the forces of evil, so vividly and graphically portrayed in His unveiling, thrill the soul with admiring wonder and adoring worship, because they teach us that the victory of virtue, the triumph of truth, and the reign of righteousness are absolutely assured. He greatly deserves the grandly designed tribute of resounding praise, gladly presented by an innumerable host in the immortal heritage (Rev. 5:9; 7:9).

A God-honoring, holy life supplies the head that wears the crown with a triumphant death. Enemies of the Cross rage most against those who are doing best and most for Christ.

THE JUST ONE

Which of the prophets have not your fathers persecuted? and they have slain them which shewed before of the coming of the Just One; of whom ye have been now the betrayers and murderers: who have received the law by the disposition of angels, and have not kept it (Acts 7:52-53).

Stephen the martyr presented to the Jewish national leaders in Jerusalem a masterful rehearsal of Old Testament history, in the light of the revealed will of God. The main lesson of his message set forth the absolute sovereignty of God's purpose for mankind, and the certainty of its being fulfilled. As Stephen portrays, the Amorites in Abraham's day may assail it, Joseph's brethren may jeopardize his life in resisting it, Pharaoh might determine with the utmost resolution of his power to prevent it, but all such opposition and obduracy succumbs to the ceaseless march of God's omnipotent will.

When concluding His comprehensive survey, Stephen reminds his hearers of the enormity of their crime, in betraying and murdering the One sent from Heaven, who was manifest for the specific purpose of fulfilling that will (John 6:38), whom he speaks of as the Just One. Stephen was familiar with the prophets as is apparent from his glowing summary of Old Testament history. Zephaniah had declared concerning Jerusalem: "The just Lord is in the midst thereof; He will not do iniquity" (Zeph. 3:5). Zechariah had proclaimed the fact to the same city of Jerusalem: "Behold, thy King cometh unto thee: He is just, and having salvation" (Zech. 9:9). Isaiah had contributed a similar testimony: "There is no God else beside Me; a just God and a Saviour" (Is. 45:21).

Our Saviour's unblemished character is attested from every quarter, and His unblighted conduct receives overwhelming testimony from a whole cloud of witnesses. The uprightness of all His dealings and the unblemished rectitude of all His deeds occupy the entire records of the four Gospels. He never once misjudges any matter, or miscalculates any motive, or misunderstands any case of need, or misappropriates any posses-

sion, or misuses any privilege, or mismanages any undertaking, or misstates any subject He taught. He is perfectly just
in estimating the value of labor and in remunerating the work
of His servants. He takes fully into account the endowment the
worker receives, the environment in which he labors, and the
energy expended in the task. He is always just in His recognition of virtue, in His remembrance of trials endured and
troubles encountered, and suitably recompenses every worthy
project achieved. He justly rewards martyrdom in the ranks of
service and recognizes the sacrificial suffering of His people,
for He experienced these things Himself. He is wholly just in
dealing with nations, races, classes, and creeds, He is fully
aware of the origin, occasion, and outcome of all such matters
and movements. His foresight, insight, and oversight enable
Him to justly view and judiciously voice His verdict in every
realm of relationship and responsibility.

All men and movements everywhere are accountable to Him
and must needs give an account of the things done in the body,
whether they be good or bad, for we must all appear before
the judgment seat of Christ (2 Cor. 5:10). If we have
misdirected men by false teaching, or denied the reality of
things unseen before members of our own family, we shall be
called to account for so doing, as the Pharisee was in our
Lord's teaching on the unjust steward (Luke 16). How is it
possible for the unjust to stand before the tribunal of the Just
One without being condemned? What a need we all have of
being justified by the justice of the Justifier. No case will be
mistried and no judgment misapplied for the Holy One and
Just reveres righteousness, and rightly regards truth. Justice
and judgment are the foundations of His throne.

His name grows in its greatness and glows in its grandeur
ever more gloriously as we proceed to investigate its inherent
wealth and intrinsic worth of merit. No name is more wondrous in prophecy, more famous in history, more lustrous in
chivalry, more generous in liberality, more gracious in
ministry, and more meritorious in the heavenly sanctuary than
the name of Jesus.

This Just One performs the most notable act of submission

in sacrifice to save us, He provides the most suitable aid that infinite strength can supply to sustain us, and He pursues the most creditable aim of service in seeking to perfect that which concerns us, to the praise of the Father's glory. None is more desirable and more adorable than He.

A JEW

How is it that Thou, being a Jew, askest drink of me, which am a woman of Samaria? (John 4:9)

The occasion of this name being used, with its historic setting beside Jacob's well in Samaria, was intended as a reproach, but it led to a research, with the discovery of a priceless treasure, namely, the true secret of life. The very associations of the locality, the arrangements made for that hour, the arrival of the woman, the appeal of Jesus for a drink, and the arrogant answer received—all are attended with higher influences, and fraught with greater issues than appear on the surface. The question, "How is it that Thou being a Jew," is followed later by the opposite party, with an assertion of sheer contempt, "Thou art a Samaritan" (John 8:48). The pronoun *thou* in each case is emphatic, supposing to add the smart of disdain by the emphasis. "Consider Him that endured such contradiction of sinners against Himself" (Heb. 12:3). "When He was reviled, [He] reviled not again" (1 Pet. 2:23). Was it ever so in Israel? Yea, a Jew, but there was never another like Him.

Saul the philosopher said, "He is not a Jew, which is one outwardly . . . but he is a Jew, which is one inwardly . . . whose praise [Judah] is not of men, but of God" (Rom. 2:28-29). The inward nature, not the outward nationality, counts most with God. The tone and temper of His nature is crystal clear and this is true of all His teaching and treatment of others. Take particular notice of His deportment in the Gospels. If they repel Him, He does not rebel; He sadly departs with deep regret (Matt. 8:34). If they reject Him, He does not object; He slowly retires with tear-filled eyes (Luke 19:41). If they deny Him, He does not demur; He glances gravely with heart-pained grief (Luke 22:61). If they scorn Him, He does not scold; He gently withdraws and sweetly smiles. If they smite Him, He does not strive; He quietly stands in serene silence (Luke 22:64). If they betray Him, He does not brandish a sword; He asks in such a case about the misuse of a kiss (Luke 22:48). If they mock Him, He does not murmur; He briefly prays, "Father, forgive them; for they know not what they do" (Luke 23:34).

Jesus accepted the title *Jew* as a compliment, and said to the one who used it, "Salvation is of the Jews" (John 4:22). So it behooves us never to speak slightingly of the Jew. He was fully conscious then and there of being the source and security of saving grace. As to His being a Jew, He is the priceless Jewel that exceeds all gems, the precious Pearl that excels all purity, and the perfect Beryl that eclipses all beauty. He who is the Judge of all, and the Justifier of the guilty, as well as being Jehovah the Just One, meets a jaded Samaritan woman jettisoned from society. Will He administer justice and condemn, or freely and frankly justify the godless one? To do the latter will cost Him more.

This is a picture of Deity unveiled in the presence of disaffected indulgence. The physical thirst of the woman is symptomatic of her inner longing for heart satisfaction. Jesus firstly appeals to her courtesy by requesting a drink; secondly He attracts her curiosity by telling her He has a great secret which she should know; thirdly He announces the calamity of her life and eventually wins her confidence and confession, thereby securing her salvation. Ah, yes, He is a teacher, a Jew, and more; a Samaritan verily. A friend? In very deed. A prophet, yea and I say unto you, more than a prophet. Was ever grace like Thine?

Wherefore ye arbiters of taste, ye conveners of fashion, ye editors of the press, know this: He is more than a teacher. Ye staunch nationalists, ye proud racialists, ye ardent ritualists, know thou He is much more than a Jew. Ye credited humanitarians, ye cultured socialists, ye considerate philanthropists, be assured of this: He is much more than a good Samaritan and social benefactor. Yes, a Jew, but possessing superhuman knowledge and understanding. A Jew, but One that wields the scepter of saving grace with an almighty hand. A Jew, but justly wearing the miter of mercy on His majestic brow, the great High Priest over the house of God. A Jew, despised and rejected of men, yet with all authority in Heaven and on earth. A Jew greater than Abraham, greater than David, greater than Solomon and all the renowed of the centuries. A Jew, yet omniscient, omnipotent, and omnipresent. A Jew, a Man of our humanity, the one Mediator between God and men, the Man Christ Jesus. A Jew, but One whose glory was great and high in creation, whose glory was greater and higher in revelation, but whose glory was greatest and highest in manifestation, when He came for the eternal purpose of mediation. The highest act of His Godhead was witnessed in the lowliest humility of His childhood (Luke 2:14). At the right hand of the Majesty on high sits an Advocate with the Father, Jesus Christ the righteous. He is the faithful Witness, and more, He is a Prince and a Saviour.

Most surely as Simeon predicted, "Behold, this child is set for the fall and rising again of many in Israel: and for a sign which shall be spoken against" (Luke 2:34). So then Jesus the First is worthy of our faith, Jesus the Truth is worthy of our trust, Jesus the Christ is worthy of our confidence, Jesus the Priest is worthy of our prayer and praise (Ps. 71:15). Let us render to Him the reverence due to His righteousness, the honor due to His holiness, and the worship due to His worthiness. Jesus the Just One, the Judge, and Justifier founded a throne of sovereignty, and established an everlasting kingdom not by force of arms, but by the fruit of the Spirit, even the fidelity of love. He fully demonstrated the sympathetic warmth of that kingdom by the love that seeks, the joy that finds, the grace that pardons, and the heart that receives into everlasting habitations. The supremest demonstration of His Sovereignty was beheld in the self-abnegating Sacrifice of Calvary, in the light of which nothing is impossible with Him.

JESUS THE KING

And sitting down they watched Him there; and set up over His head His accusation written, This is Jesus the King of the Jews (Matt. 27:36).
A superscription also was written over Him in letters of Greek, and Latin, and Hebrew (Luke 23:38).

The inquiry made by the Wise Men when they reached Jerusalem is recorded in Matthew 2:2; "Where is He that is born King of the Jews? for we have seen His star in the east, and are come to worship Him." The climax reached in the earthly career of this worthy One is tragic, for He was crucified on a brutal cross and above His head stood the accusation, This is Jesus, the King of the Jews. Luke the beloved physician tells us that the title was written in three languages, while Matthew says it was intended as an accusation. Pilate, however, without comprehending what he had done, wrote a wonderful commendation.

Greek was noted as the language of culture, Latin of control, and Hebrew of covenant. In what sense, may we ask, did these facts make any contribution to the distinguished character and mission of Jesus, the King of the Jews? In the first place, in the matter of culture, we know that He came down from Heaven to bring to man the knowledge of God, a knowledge, He declared, no one else possessed (Matt. 11:27). Secondly, in regard to control, He came to proclaim the kingdom of God and this was the subject of His preaching (Matt. 4:17). Thirdly, in relation to covenants, He came to express the kindness of God, as Paul wrote, "After that the kindness and love of God our Saviour toward man appeared" (Titus 3:4). This great compact was ratified by a sacrifical act to which our Saviour referred when He said, "This cup is the new covenant in My blood, even that which is poured out for you" (Luke 22:20 ASV).

So the superscription signified much more than Pilate intended, for in relation to these three significant languages, the writing conveyed and confirmed the complete character of Messiah's ministry, and indicated that He represented the highest knowledge, the heavenly kingdom, and the holiest kindness. No other representative from any realm whatsoever had appeared in this world for such a divine and dignified purpose.

When we contemplate Christ as the expression of the Father, we naturally think of His countenance. His face was the loveliest feature ever seen, from whence was reflected the light of the knowledge of the glory of God (2 Cor. 4:6). "We beheld His glory, the glory as of the only begotten of the Father."

As for the exhibition of power, we are immediately reminded of His competence, for He exercised power over all the power of the enemy, and over all flesh. He demonstrated His control over the material, physical, spiritual, and judicial domains. His personal claim to power is all-inclusive: "As the Father raiseth up the dead, and quickeneth them; even so the Son quickeneth whom He will." Again: "As the Father hath life in Himself; so hath He given to the Son to have life in Himself; and hath given Him authority to execute judgment also, because He is the Son of man" (John 5:26-27). He exercised the strongest power ever wielded in this world.

In regard to the establishment of the covenant, we at once reflect on the compassion of the Saviour. The word *compassion* is used of Jesus on six occasions in the Gospels, as demonstrating His attitude toward the dire needs of mankind. This word means much more than sympathy with the sorrow-stricken; it refers to that heart-rending, soul-stirring, deep-seated pity that intelligently senses man's helpless state. This it was that drew out His devotion and caused Him to dedicate Himself to make the supreme sacrifice to remove the cause of human grief. His was the richest grace ever beheld and the noblest virtue ever displayed.

These three activities constitute the infallible proof, the indelible mark, and the ineffable sign that He was all He claimed to be, in that He reveals God, represents God, and ratifies God's covenant. This certainly is Jesus the King.

What He taught and testified by His words and witness was absolutely in accord with the eternal Father's character.

He lived and labored in full harmony with the designs and decisions of the divine dominion.

He had served and sacrificed in perfect agreement with the will and wisdom of God.

Wherefore the entire manifestation, ministry, and mediation of the Saviour exemplified the three great features, namely, the knowledge of God, the kingdom of God, and the kindness of God. What further need have we of witness, that this is Jesus the King of the Jews.

> I love to sing of Christ my King
> And hail Him blessed Jesus;
> The sweetest word ear ever heard,
> That name, the name of Jesus.

JEHOVAH OF HOSTS

Thus saith Jehovah, the King of Israel, and His Redeemer, Jehovah of hosts: I am the first, and I am the last; and beside Me there is no God [Saviour] (Isa. 44:6 ASV).

The profound and awesome title *Jehovah,* which is mostly rendered by the word *Lord* in the Authorized Version, is used 7,600 times in the Scriptures and is definitely applied to Jesus Christ our Saviour and Lord. We may confidently say in the light of this wonderful designation that the Bible as a book is the revelation of the name. In the Greek language there is no equivalent for this Hebrew title; therefore, whenever a quotation in which it occurs is made from the Old Testament, the word *Lord* is substituted. The One who affirmed five times over in the book of the Revelation, "I AM the first and the last," added further confirmation of His identity with the name *Jehovah* by also declaring on four occasions in the unveiling, "I am Alpha and Omega." The use here made of the first and last letters in the Greek alphabet not only corroborates the statement of our heading, but the letters also comprise the two vowels used in the Hebrew word *Jehovah.*

Wherefore, Jesus is Jehovah. Notice, John the forerunner of

Jesus was to go before the face of Jehovah to prepare His ways
(Luke 1:76 Newberry).

Jehovah is the age-abiding, all-pervading One, who, in His
eternal being, inhabits eternity. Our finite minds falter when
we attempt to comprehend that the repository of infinite
wisdom, the residence of infinite power, and the reservoir of
infinite love are centered in the intrinsic holiness of the Christ,
bodily (Col. 2:9). This magnificent name, *Jehovah*, incorporates every capacity conceivable of creative ability,
redemptive activity, and mediative authority. All the benefits
and blessings emanating from such attributes have been made
available to man through the manifestation and mediation of
Jesus, which title in Hebrew means "Jehovah saves."
Wherefore, in Jesus the Saviour we are able to comprehend the
incomprehensible, and know the unknowable, because He
verifies the invisible realities.

We remember that under the old economy the lights and
perfections of the adorable name *Jehovah* were made known to
Israel through the medium of Urim and Thummim, which appeared on the breastplate worn by the high priest (Ex.
28—30). That which would otherwise have been hidden in
mystery concerning God's justice and judgments was made
known through the breastplate worn over Aaron's heart. Urim
means lights, and Thummim, perfections, indicating that
Jehovah's character consists of lights and perfections, in whom
is no darkness at all, and whose entire nature is absolutely free
of all imperfection. The instruction contained in this teaches
us that the true character of Deity is expressed most clearly in
the righteousness of His judgments. Even His mercy is based
on His justice.

> Jesus bruised and put to shame
> Tells me all Jehovah's name,
> God is love I surely know
> By my Saviour's depth of woe.
>
> R. C. CHAPMAN

When Christ was made to be sin for us, God spared not His
own Son. The stroke of justice fell on Him, so as another hymn

writer states: "The heart of God is revealed at the Cross." The words of Psalm 85 reflect the same truth (verses 10-13). "Jehovah-jireh," said Abraham, "in the mount of the Lord it shall be seen"; and so it proved at Mount Calvary. The perfection of God's justice assures the protection of justification.

The Lord said to Moses, "I am the Lord [Jehovah Ropheka] that healeth thee" (Ex. 15:26). What consolation! "Who healeth all thy diseases"; "Himself took our infirmities"; "the sun of righteousness shall arise with healing in His wings"; "up from the grave He arose, with a mighty triumph o'er His foes." The leaves of this tree are for the health of the nations (Rev. 22:2).

Moses called the name of the place Jehovah-nissi, Jehovah my banner (Ex. 17:15). "His banner over me is love," unfurled on the field of battle where the inveterate enemy of God's people was judged. Our Lord when speaking of His cross said, "Now is the judgment of this world: now shall the prince of this world be cast out" (John 12:31). The great triumph of the Cross in subduing principalities and powers is plainly stated in Colossians 2:14-15.

Gideon contributes a further aspect by calling the altar he built Jehovah-shalom, the peace of Jehovah. So likewise peace has been made through the blood of the Cross (Col. 1:20). Justice appointed a victim to be slain, approved of the sacrifice, and accepted as propitiation the offering of one perfect life. The peace of God which surpasseth understanding is available, for He is our peace (Eph. 2:14).

In view of the crucifixion portrayed in Psalm 22:14-18, David addresses the Saviour as Jehovah Rohi, Jehovah my Shepherd (Ps. 23:1). So Christ affirms: "I am the good shepherd: the good shepherd layeth down His life for the sheep" (John 10:11 ASV). Compare Psalm 22:26 with John 10:27. How competent He is to sustain, beneath me, green pastures; beside me, still waters; before me, a prepared table; behind me, goodness and mercy; between me, the valley of the shadow; and beyond, the house of the Lord forever.

Jeremiah the prophet tells of the King reigning and prospering, executing judgment and justice in the earth, who secures salvation and stability and His name is called Jehovah Tsid-kenu, which means, Jehovah our righteousness.

The full and final revelation of these fascinating features of the Godhead and as many more contained in the remaining compound titles, made use of in the Old Testament, are all realized superlatively in the person of Jesus Christ our Lord. The ineffable beauty of His lambent life, the brilliance of His effulgent light, and the brightness of His radiant luster express the complete character of Godhead and exhibit the crowning compliment of God's glorious grace. In Him we find the replete revelation of the gospel of the blessed God. All the nobility of the Deity is clearly seen, the comeliness of the Divine Character is displayed, and the holiness of the Highest is presented perfectly. Jehovah-Jesus is the Just and the Justifier, the Originator of creation, the Ordainer of redemption, the Overcomer of the world, and the Overseer of God's house. Through Him we have been made heirs of hopes too lofty and too lovely for them ever to prove false. They could never have been the product of human thinking, because they are too grand to have been conceived in the heart of man (1 Cor. 2:9). The perfectly blended beauties in the character of this beloved bridegroom of our hearts, who bought us at infinite cost, have blessings in store beyond our present capacity to comprehend. However, we do know that when He shall appear, we shall be like Him, righteous, radiant, and refined, bearing His image and wearing His likeness.

JAH

> Sing unto God, sing praises to His name: extol Him that rideth upon the heavens by His name Jah (Ps. 68:4).

Jah, as a title, is also rendered *Yah,* and in these two forms appears forty-nine times in the Old Testament, being confined in its use to three books, those of Exodus, Psalms, and Isaiah. Moses the man of God is the first to make mention of it in his memorable song, "The Lord [Jah] is my strength and song" (Ex. 15:2). The name is made up of the first and last letters of the title *Jehovah*, which are linked together with one of its two vowels. A word so simple and yet so strikingly suggestive of the sublime and eternal One. Here the initial and the infinite combine in a monosyllabic name. Even in the holiest form of heavenly adoration on high, the title rings out in the use made of the word *Hallelujah*, which means, "Praise ye Yah," and is rendered in our version, "Praise ye the Lord." Twenty-six times it appears in this form, in the book of Psalms. Wonderful indeed that the divine entity of personality and eternity of being should be wrapped up in so small a compass.

The superb hymn from whence our heading is quoted is unsurpassed in the grandeur of its sustained stream of triumphant praise. The subject depicts the incalculable victory of God, which follows His inconceivable campaign of conquest through the immeasurable spaces of infinitude, which are termed "the heavens of heavens" (verse 33), and His reentry into the celestial sanctuary from whence He came. When we read that Jesus ascended up far above all heavens that He might fill all things, our minds instinctively turn to this psalm, which depicts the scene most graphically and describes Christ's ascension as attended with twenty thousand chariots and thousands of angels (verses 17-18). Amazing thought that this One, majestic in might, is seen in the next psalm so overwhelmed with reproach that His heart is broken (Ps. 69:9-10,19-20).

On two occasions Isaiah the prophet uses the title *Jah* in association with strength and song, as did Moses. He declares the Lord to be most worthy of trust, for, says he, "In the Lord Jehovah [Jah Jehovah] is everlasting strength" (Isa. 26:4). He shows that the title signifies unchallengeable strength, and unchanging love, which are the characteristics of the One who is the mainstay of defense. Dr. Toplady, in his universal hymn, rightly renders the picturesque beauty of the meaning attached to the title in this verse, "Rock of Ages." If we examine the context of the vision which begins in chapter 24, we find that no class escapes the avalanche that overtakes mankind (verse 2). The one great objective of the divine activity is to head up all things in Christ. Wherefore, in chapter 25 the great triumph is gained by the coming of the Lord, and death is swallowed up in victory. Paul the apostle quotes this statement in His great discourse on eschatology (1 Cor. 15:54). We have cause to wonder how anyone could possibly be maintained in perfect peace at such a time of universal upheaval and overthrow. But we are assured that peace is by divine ordination (Isa. 26:12). This is followed by a colorful picture of how the guarantee is fulfilled: "Come, My people, enter thou into thy chambers, and shut thy doors about thee: hide thyself as it were for a little moment, until the indignation be overpast" (Isa. 26:20).

The prophet directs us to the character of the hiding place later, and describes that a man, a king, a rock unfailing is our refuge (Isa. 32:1-2). So then, it is the mystery of the miraculous might of Jah Jehovah, that sublimely noble and overpowering title, that secures serenity. Jah Himself is the Bastion of defense, the Bulwark of security, the Fastness of Safety, and the Citadel of steadfast protection. Because He is immutably the same we are immortally safe. Jah is the absolute One of infinite ability, the magnificent One of majestic might, and the superior One of stately strength. This name of His stands out conspicuously as a signal of staunchness, and a sign of steadfastness. We are confident of our guardian Caretaker, because He is Champion in the field of strength, might, and power. That is why even today if we wait upon Him we renew our strength. Our association with such a sovereign is based assuredly on His atoning sacrifice, for peace was made through the blood of His cross. We have been translated into His kingdom and can rest and feast and trust. For the enjoying of His matchless presence, we are to be at home in the high noon of Heaven's summertide, with hearts in harmony with the Highest, as Christ taught, "Ye shall be children of the Highest." Paul contemplated this abode, this home, this very refuge, when he said, "Your life is hid with Christ in God" (Col. 3:3). Myriads may march in their multiform ranks, and hordes of besiegers may hunt for spoils, but they cannot break the tranquil calm of His chosen ones. "We have a strong city," a stronger Christ, a Super-caretaker, for

Jah is both Governor and Guardian, garrisoning the mind with peace that surpasseth all understanding. Well might we exult in Him and exclaim, Jah is my strength and song. He also is become my salvation. Hallelujah! Hallelujah!

> Moving! Yes, the world is moving
> To its dread and final end,
> Sea and shore and mountain rocking,
> Soon the last great trump shall rend.
>
> Moving with unerring footsteps
> Is the superhuman race,
> Every soul of man is hast'ning
> On to his eternal place.
>
> On where creeds and sects and systems
> Shall be viewed with other eyes,
> All shall stand unmasked and naked
> At the last and grand assize.
>
> Earth shall drop her mortal covering,
> Spirit meet in spirit's sphere,
> Faith itself shall loose its anchor
> When the unseen shall appear.
>
> Oh! when Heaven and earth are passing,
> Crumbling as a burning scroll,
> Is there no abiding foothold,
> No fixed refuge for the soul?
>
> Yes, a Man, the Man Christ Jesus,
> On the wreck of time He stands,
> And the souls of countless millions
> Lie within His pierced hands.

Let us learn to take our eyes off our own inability to protect ourselves and rivet them on His infinite ability. Let us resolve to look away from the lack of strength to defend, and concentrate on His divine sufficiency to safeguard from all harm and alarm. The utterances made concerning the everlasting strength of Jah are unmatched in their descriptiveness of His prevailing majesty, and are meant to supply every reason for strong confidence, come what may. His safe retreat and sure refuge are strong to withstand any onslaught. We should rejoice greatly, because Jah is in Himself an impregnable Fortress, an impenetrable Fastness, and an imperishable Fullness to furnish every facility for the maintenance of the hosts secured. Let us slightly change the stanza of the familiar hymn and lustily sing,

> Rock of ages, cleft for me,
> I am hidden, Jah, in Thee.

K

The case is wholly relevant, that He who is so ancient and valiant should bear the most excellent and transcendent of names in the entire universe.

The KINSMAN (Ruth 2:14)
>   The rights of relationship.

The KINDNESS OF GOD (Titus 3:4)
>   The revealed heart of the Highest Himself.

The KEEPER OF ISRAEL (Ps. 121:3-5)
>   The reliable Protector and resolute Preserver.

The KING (Is. 33:17)
>   The Celebrity of competent control.

The KING OF THE JEWS (Matt. 2:2)
>   The clearest credentials of claim.

The KING OF ISRAEL (John 1:49)
>   The conditions of the covenant confirmed.

The KING OF SAINTS (Rev. 15:3)
>   The scepter of sanctity and sublimity.

The KING OF THE AGES (1 Tim. 1:17)
>   The Assurer of abiding authority.

The KING OF RIGHTEOUSNESS (Heb. 7:1-3)
>   Matchless in His majestic might.

The KING OF HEAVEN (Dan. 4:37)
>   The very Essence of eternal excellency.

The KING OF GLORY (Ps. 24:7)
>   Princeliest in perfection and power.

The KING OF KINGS (Rev. 19:12)
>   The kingliest in royalty and regality.

THE PRINCE OF THE KINGS
OF THE EARTH

Christ the Racial King	(Matt. 2:2)
Christ the National King	(John 1:49)
Christ the Ecclesiastical King	(Rev. 14:3,4)
Christ the Spiritual King	(Heb. 7:1-3)
Christ the Historical King	(1 Tim. 1:17)
Christ the Celestial King	(Dan. 4:37)
Christ the Supernal King	(Ps. 24:7-8)

THE KING OF KINGS

Title of titles, the King of all kings,
　Hailing thy triumphs a multitude sings,
Glorified millions greet Thee, the Lord!
　Grand in Thy splendor, all Heaven is awed.

Highest and noblest, famous Thy crowns,
　Greatest in honor, Thy pleasure abounds.
Preciously perfect, glorious Thy face,
　Righteous in justice, yet choicest in grace.

Majesty magnified! noblest as Heir,
　Stately thy kingship, so wondrously fair.
Comely Thy countenance, shining as light,
　Holy in beauty and matchlessly bright.

Peerless and charming Thy beauteous name
　Cheers with its melody, brighter than flame.
Resounding clearest, and thrilling great throngs,
　Thy name Lord Jesus is sweeter than songs.

Friendly and constant, faithful and true,
　Reigning in power, creating anew;
Harmony everywhere, great is Thy peace,
　Christly Thy majesty, bringing release.

Wonderful fragrance, Thy name is sublime,
Richest in perfume, a savor divine;
Redolent praise blessed Lord be to Thee,
Ruling in splendor by yon crystal sea.

                            C. J. R.

I am Alpha and Omega (Rev. 22:13)

The character of Christ is magnificent from every angle, His name has an exclusive distinction that is unparalleled, and His fame ranks highest in an excellence of dignity that is unequalled in the whole realm of knowledge. The immutability of His essential Godhead is indicated by the statement that inherently He obtained a more excellent name than angelic beings, which are a creation (Heb. 1:4). Likewise, the name by which He was to be known at His manifestation was determined ere creation dawned, and the fullness of its meaning was definitely designed. The omniscient decision was made in the counsels of the ages that He should have a Name above every name, the most ancient and valiant. So that we know that in both revelation and reality He bears a Name that stands highest, and which in majesty and holiness is the most resplendent, in memory and hope the most radiant, in mastery and honor the most regnant, and in mercy and help the most relevant.

He has demonstrated His reliability in the ratification of immutable covenants and in keeping them honorably, in pledging imperishable promises and fulfilling them worthily, and in assuring unfailing maintenance for His church and providing it lavishly. The administrative power He wields in governing the universe, the representative function He undertakes in revealing the Father and the protective office He holds in safeguarding His redeemed people, unanimously verify the integrity and fidelity of His worthy name. Both the durable nature of His dominion over creation and the desirable manner of His administration captivate soul interest because of His competency, and draw from the heart a reverent adoration.

We need but contemplate the silent majesty of the sun so

grandly impressive, the swaying leagues of azure skies with their impenetrable spaces, the spacious heavens and cloudy vaults with their ever-changing mists, the stellar magnitudes untouched by human hands, scintillating their myriad starry beauties across the bosom of eternity to form the vestibule of God's temple in the Heaven of heavens, and we bow in wonder as we worship the Controller of such magnificent handiwork. When we view the silvery stillness of dawn mirroring the loveliness of celestial perfection, the solemnizing sunsets so gorgeously golden and colorfully blended, the stately array of massive trees in forest glades with their rich ringlets of foliage, the stormy winds in their ceaseless whirlings and limitless range, and dwell on the secret remoteness of the ineffable glory that stretches beyond the range of telescopic vision, we need reminding that such profound features, and all else that is visible, are going to wax old as doth a garment and as a vesture they shall be changed; but He abideth, He endureth, He remaineth forever the same (Heb. 1:10,12). These credentials of His creatorship fully identify His almighty power, magnify His superior personality, amplify the enduring sovereignty of His authority, and glorify the noble dignity of His majesty. The ethical standards He set are the highest, the moral virtues He expressed are the holiest, the spiritual perfections He exhibited are the heavenliest ever witnessed on earth.

The conception of a character such as Christ so completely perfect requires a perfect mind, and one with a perfect mind would never impose an imperfect administration on His creation. The Scriptures assert, "As for God, His way is perfect" (Ps. 18:30). On the strength of this David said with confidence: "He will perfect that which concerneth me," and again, "He maketh my way perfect" (verse 32).

In the biography we have of Christ's life, which was communicated by the Spirit of truth, there is not the slightest suggestion of a reserved aspect having been kept back because of its being undesirable. Our Lord never once spoke a regrettable word that needed recalling. Not one recorded deed that He wrought was unworthy of the claims He made. No remark He ever passed was unkind, no rebuke He uttered was unwarranted, no reproof He expressed was uncalled for, and no reason He gave at any time in defense of His methods was unwise. He always and everywhere upheld the honor of the holy name by which He was called.

His behavior at the wedding in Cana of Galilee as Son of Mary (John 2:1), His resounding command at the grave of Lazarus as Son of God (John 11), His deportment at the triumphant entry as Son of David (John 12:13), and the manner in which He conducted Himself when contemplating the Cross as Son of man (John 12:23), emblazons His name on the annals of history for all time as the most distinguished personality the world has ever known.

Christ brought into this world a new courtesy of love, a new constancy of life, and a new category of light. He bore witness to the delights of a celestial home, the domain of a corruptless heritage, and the dominion of a Christian kingdom that abides forever. We now turn to consider twelve of Christ's titles commencing with the letter K.

THE KINSMAN

> Blessed be the Lord, which hath not left thee this day without a kinsman, that his name may be famous in Israel. And he shall be unto thee a restorer of thy life, and a nourisher of thine old age (Ruth 4:14-15).

The kinsman or goel of the Bible fulfilled a very important function in the national life of Israel in the matters of a death in the home or a debt on the heritage or both. A young widow had the right to request help from the brother of her deceased husband, and such a one was legally bound to respond and render the aid necessary. This duty was not always considered an honor; sometimes it was rather humiliating. In the main it was a great boon, and in its message there is no richer blessing derived than in the results secured on account of Christ's undertaking to fulfill the kinsman's part for the welfare of humanity.

In the case in point, Ruth had fallen upon evil days. She returned with her mother-in-law from the land of Moab, where Naomi had resided for several years. The estate of

Ruth's deceased husband was already in the hand of a stranger. When Boaz ascertained the facts of the case he determined to undertake the duties of a kinsman on behalf of Ruth, the widow from Moab. The first requirement on the part of Boaz was to substantiate his right to undertake the task. Having done so, he was required to vindicate the law by discharging certain obligations. Then he must needs liquidate the debt on the estate. Following this he was to consummate the union by marrying Ruth.

Wherefore, if Christ was to become the Saviour of the world He must first of all substantiate His right on the ground of relationship to man, for no stranger or foreigner was permitted to act. Christ therefore came into manifestation as Son of man and in this capacity He is related to all men. Man had forfeited his right and title to the world as his estate. In the next step, Christ undertook to vindicate the law, for the law was holy. This He did by fulfilling all legal demands, yea, He magnified the law and made it honorable. The third requirement was to liquidate the debt in order to redeem man and ransom the estate. This He did fully, justly, and finally.

One other transaction awaits achievement. He must come and take His bride and consummate the eternal union, and receive her into the Father's house on high. The four Gospels represent Christ fulfilling these great functions. In Matthew He substantiates His right to redeem by His universal name and His unblemished nature. His genealogy is traced, His relationship ratified, and the documentary evidence is supplied. In Mark He vindicates the law and in so doing encounters the usurper who dominated the heritage, and who mars it by demon possession, sickness, social dislocation, and poisons. In Luke's Gospel Christ is portrayed liquidating the debt to make the bankrupt solvent, liberating the captives and setting them free, while in John's message we read, "He that hath the bride is the bridegroom." So He is expected to return and consummate the union. Our Lord therefore is first the Kinsman, then the Avenger, the Redeemer, and the Bridegroom.

In these four functions the Gospels express the majesty of His person, the mastery of His prerogative, the ministry of His purchase, and the mystery of His purpose. Nor are we left in any doubt as to the final consummation of His great and gracious purpose, for in the book of the Revelation the four official duties are more fully presented and faithfully discharged. The Kinsman occupies the first three chapters, and in His character as Son of man He is seen in His kinsman relationship as connected with all kindreds of the earth.

In chapters 4 to 7 He is described as the Avenger, and the martyred saints say in their appeal, "How long, O Lord, holy and true, dost Thou not judge and avenge our blood on them that dwell on the earth?" (Rev. 6:10) In chapters 8 to 13 Christ is the Redeemer of the heritage, and the kingdoms of this world become the kingdom of our Lord and of His Christ (11:15). In the closing section, chapters 14 to 22, Christ is the Bridegroom and calls His bride to the marriage supper.

Whatever else of His offices and oversight are unveiled, these four great functions cannot be denied. This Hebrew law of redemption in Israel, enacted so methodically by the Kinsman, spans the whole Bible from Deuteronomy 25 to the end of the New Testament. The book of Ruth supplies, by illustration, a complete outline in miniature of this matchless purpose. No portraiture of Christ is more heartening than when we examine and exult in His acknowledged affinity to all mankind, His absolute authority to master the usurper, His amazing activity to mitigate the debt, and His administrative ability to make all things new in an eternal home for the bride. The changeless dignity of Christ's personal charm, the comely beauty of His virtue, the constant courtesy of His love, the cheerful majesty of His feature, and the crowning glory of His grace combine in their manifold wealth to set Him loftily above all other claimants, as Kinsman, Avenger, Redeemer, Bridegroom.

THE KINSMAN-REDEEMER

To verify His right He came,
  To demonstrate His friendly Name
The Son of man drew nigh to all
  Who had been ruined by the Fall.

In sympathy His heart drew near
　　To seek and save from sin and fear,
The Father sent Him from above
　　To demonstrate His perfect love.

To vindicate the law He came,
　　To save His own from death and shame
He undertook the tragic case,
　　Was made a curse to free our race.
And now no charge can e'er be laid,
　　For He, in all, full payment made.
God's righteousness is now our dress,
　　The fairest robes of spotlessness.

To liquidate our debt He came,
　　To free mankind of guilt and blame,
To pay in full the ransom due
　　And all the joys of life renew.
No plumes of pomp or gaudy crown
　　Are needed to secure renown,
He loved the Church, let this suffice,
　　He gave Himself to pay the price.

To consummate a union firm
　　Not for a season or a term,
But one that lasts throughout the years,
　　All free of sorrow, pain, and tears,
He comes again, and will unite
　　In bonds of love and life and light,
The Bride from whom He bled and died,
　　In mansions with the glorified.

　　　　　　　　　　　　　　C. J. R.

THE KINDNESS OF GOD

> After that the kindness and love of God our Saviour toward man appeared, not by works of righteousness which we have done, but according to His mercy He saved us, by the washing of regeneration, and renewing of the Holy Ghost (Titus 3:4-5).

Kindness is love's considerate compassion as such; love suffereth long and is kind. God is love, and God is kindness; Christ expresses and exemplifies both in His own person. "For the mountains shall depart, and the hills be removed; but My kindness shall not depart from thee, neither shall the covenant of My peace be removed, saith the Lord that hath mercy on thee" (Isa. 54:10). The kindness of God as exemplified in Christ abides forever: "With everlasting kindness will I have mercy on thee, saith the Lord, Thy [kinsman] redeemer" (verse 8 Newberry margin). By virtue of kindness as a medium, we identify love, wherefore we are exhorted to be kind one to another as the proof of our love (Eph. 4:32).

The love that existed between David and Jonathan is proverbial. After Jonathan's death on the hills of Gilboah, King David resolved to find out if there were any of his late comrade's descendants remaining, to whom he might show the kindness of God for Jonathan's sake (2 Sam. 9:3) as a means of keeping the memory of his faithful friend fresh and fragrant.

One son was discovered, as unattractive and unwinsome as any in Israel, and he was well aware of his own unloveliness and spoke of himself as being a dead dog. This was a true test to prove if David's desire was real. What wonderful kindness David showed to Jonathan's son, Mephibosheth, throughout the remainder of his life, not by giving him a memento as a memorial of his deceased father, but by ministering daily kindness.

Christ personifies the kindness of God, and His treatment of mankind is too amazing to express. We were all as an unclean thing, unholy, unrighteous, undeserving, yea, ungodly. We were devoid of all merit and destitute of all credit, and yet, in the fullness of time, the splendor of His kindness and the favor of His love appeared. The mute appeal of our misery moved Him to consider our case, and God gave His best to lay down His life for the worst. His life was of more value than all other lives in one, yet He loved me. David could say of Jonathan, "Thy love to me was wonderful." Say it again, He loved me! even me! For this ineffably lovely One to appear among the deceitful, the distasteful, the disgraceful sons of men seems so uncalled for, entirely unmerited, and even unsought. Why make so noble a sacrifice for such ignoble creatures? Never was kindness so fully displayed and so clearly defined.

The unusual kindness of Boaz toward Ruth and the unselfish kindness of Ruth toward Naomi (Ruth 2:20; 3:10), together with the unstinted kindness of David toward Mephibosheth, are but minor illustrations of the more memorable kindness of God in Christ Jesus toward mankind. In the latter of the three, the personal beauty and princely deformity and pitiable impotency of the cripple he befriended. The same contrasts are depicted in greater degree among those addressed at Ephesus, who were dead in trespasses and sins, but quickened, raised, and seated in the heavenlies with the King of Heaven. One of the masterpieces of divine grace to be exhibited in the ages to come will be His kindness toward us through Christ Jesus (Eph. 2:7). Truly, as recorded in the Psalms, "His merciful kindness is great toward us" (Ps. 117:2).

Never before in world history did regal kingliness and real kindliness meet so perfectly in one person. Here we observe the blended beauty of loveliness and lowliness, and the harmonious combination of presiding sovereignty and prevailing sympathy united in God's beloved Son. The kindly manner and kingly majesty of His deportment, the Christly courtesy and comely constancy of His demeanor transcend the radiance of the noonday sun. Spend a little time considering the expressions of His kindness in the home at Bethany, toward the widow of Nain, and in the household of Jairus, and you will find His steps were strewn with the kindness of God.

Awake, my soul, in joyful lays, and sing thy Great Redeemer's praise;
He justly claims a song from thee, His loving-kindness, oh, how free.

He saw me ruined by the Fall, yet loved me notwithstanding all;
He saved me from my lost estate, His loving-kindness, oh, how great.

* * *

Soon shall we mount and soar away,
To the bright realms of endless day,
And sing with rapture and surprise,
His loving-kindness in the skies.

SAMUEL MEDLEY

THE KEEPER OF ISRAEL

He will not suffer thy foot to be moved: He that keepeth thee will not slumber. Behold, He that keepeth Israel shall neither slumber nor sleep. The Lord is thy keeper: the Lord is thy shade upon thy right hand (Ps. 121:3-5).

The association of this heartening assurance combines, in alternating statements, six positive proofs of the Lord's protecting power, together with six negative characteristics, each one of which contributes something toward a more confident trust. No one is more desirable and affable and no one is more suitable and amiable to be a Keeper, than He.

His kindliness and kingliness are qualities that capture the sensibilities of the soul and enrapture with constant comfort and confident contentment the capacities of heart and mind.

The very character of this Keeper should forever confirm our confidence in His ability to achieve what He undertakes to do. This feature of being a keeper is first used in the Bible in connection with tending flocks; so we may safely say our Keeper is sympathetic as a shepherd with sufficiencies to sustain and strength to maintain which capabilities have been unquestionably established. Isaiah the prophet links His keeping powers with everlasting strength, and declares also that He is never weary and there is no searching of His understanding (Isa. 26:4; 40:28).

With men, keenness of understanding is not maintained without sleep, but the keeper mentioned here needs none and

He is omniscient, knowing all conditions; and He is omnipotent, capable of acting in all circumstances. Little wonder our attention is called to behold so marvelous a Preserver.

He greatly prizes His people because of what it cost Him to procure them, therefore He constantly protects them as the treasures of His royal heritage. Yea, He speaks of His own as "My jewels" and describes their dwelling place, as "a crown of glory and royal diadem," and pledges to make them an eternal excellency.

If we have any knowledge of the sedulous care expended in protecting the crown jewels of a kingdom, we are able to form some estimate of the scrupulous manner in which the Lord safeguards His people. He actually committed them to the custody of Michael, the archangel, in the wilderness (Isa. 63:9-11). As our Keeper He is never unmindful of His charge, never unattentive to a need, never unprepared to help, and can never be taken unawares by the foe. If we would like to experience an enduring consolation such as Paul refers to (2 Thess. 2:16), let us dwell extensively on His everlasting considerateness and eternal care. There can be no loneliness in the company of His loveliness, and no listlessness in the presence of His loving-kindness. We are surrounded by the favor of His covenant faithfulness, environed with the fervor of His constant friendliness, and encompassed with the fragrance of His complacent freshness, always.

> Deeper depths and higher heights,
> In wider range than comet flights,
> The dome of God's encircling love,
> Is greater than the sky above.

What radiant light is shed on the subject of security when we consider the boundless power, matchless might, and searchless strength of our Keeper. Some of the greatest expressions of the Saviour's superiority are exhibited in connection with His singular strength to save and secure His redeemed people. Such figures as majestic mountains and massive rocks, armored hills and almighty hands, and many such metaphors, are called into requisition to interpret the impregnable character of his remarkable refuge. This kingliest of Keepers by the immovability of His divine immutability maintains by virtue of His mediatorial merit and magisterial mercy the steadfast stronghold against all challenge, whether it be from material, mental, or militant power. Blessed be His name, He who never slumbers nor sleeps, giveth sleep to His beloved.

During the time of the air-raid blitz in London, one old lady who frequented a well-built dugout night after night in the heart of the city was told by two younger women that they were at a loss to know why it was she slept so soundly amid the din and uncertainty, when it was so necessary to remain on the alert. "Well," she replied, "the Lord is my Keeper and He never slumbers nor sleeps, so it is needless for the two of us to remain awake." How essential it is that we know the character of our Keeper if we would share the practical enjoyment of this quietude. An intimate knowledge of Him results in a clear conscience, a contented mind, a confident faith, and a calm spirit because He is so capable, considerate, and constant.

> Said the robin to the sparrow,
> "I should really like to know,
> Why those restless human beings
> Rush about and worry so."
>
> Said the sparrow to the robin,
> "I suppose that it must be
> They have no Heavenly Father
> Such as cares for you and me."

THE KING

Thine eyes shall see the king in his beauty: they shall behold the land that is very far off [of far distances] (Isa. 33:17 Newberry margin).

Over 2,630 references to king and kings appear on the pages of the Old Testament. There is a sense in which Christ inherited the title *King* from His identifying Himself with the house of David and tribe of Judah in the nation of Israel. Such connections, however, do by no means fully and adequately explain His kingly power and royal nature. His kingly authority is underived, His kingly majesty unconferred, and His kingly glory unimparted on the basis of this world's standards.

Christ was divinely appointed King, definitely approved by Heaven, and decidedly anointed by Deity (Ps. 2:1-7). He introduced into kingship a new mystery by wielding authority over unseen powers, a new majesty by swaying empire over disease and death, a new mastery by dominating the material, physical, social, and moral realms, and a new ministry of mercy and mediation for the needs of mankind. A further distinction of His significant jurisdiction is the fact that it is age-abiding; He knows no successor or superior and there can never be a usurper to undermine His throne of righteousness. His almighty power insures His reign against frustration of purpose, or forfeiture of principality. His credentials as a Ruler are complete, His competence as a King is perfect, and His capabilities as a Governor are of the highest caliber. All of these qualifications are totally independent of earth's temporal systems of legislation and administration.

God did not borrow the use of these terms of office, such as *kingship, sonship, heirship,* and *lordship,* from humanity; these distinctions were current in the celestial realm before man was created.

Christ, as the light of the world, brought into visibility the reality of relationships that were in operation in the realm of glory before the world was (John 17:5), of which glory Christ is King (Ps. 24:7). The kingdom of Heaven is anterior to the kingdom of Israel, for the things seen are temporal and the things unseen are eternal. Wherefore, Christ did not begin a career as a king in the present order. He was King when born into the world (Matt. 2:2).

During His ministry among men He demonstrated His kingly authority in the material, physical, infernal, mental, social, moral, spiritual, judicial, supernatural, and every other sphere known to mankind. Every law of the universe was under the control of His omnipotent hand. He had demonstrated to

Israel that He was Creator of the seasons by the character of the cropping law He gave to them (Lev. 25:1-7,20-22). During His ministry He confirmed this by His teaching in Matthew 6:25-33. He also disclosed that He was Controller of the storm and Commander of the wind (Matt. 8:25; 14:32-33). Every aspect of administration lies within the orbit of His governmental control. His word is authoritative in every realm of jurisdiction. His will is absolute in every sphere of authorization. His wisdom is authentic in His perfect workmanship everywhere. In the resources of His kingdom there is no limit, and in the height of His glory there is no summit. No utterance can go beyond His word to His disciples: "All power is given unto Me in heaven and on earth." Such an outlook is not some vague idea or vain dream, but the vital statement of a victorious King, who conquered death and has never known defeat.

The contemplation of one supreme authority with all- pervading control is a fundamental conception among great thinkers the world over. Men of various races and religions have framed their cherished ideas and ideals into a variety of systems of thought, directing them to a wonderful and worthy consummation of the existing order under a unified and single control that would eliminate national conflict, racial cleavage, class clash, creed controversy, and sex contention altogether. In the light of revelation this desire is wholly warrantable, for God has made known the mystery of His will. In the new order or dispensation, He will gather together in one all things in Christ, both which are in Heaven and which are in earth, even in Him (Eph. 1:9-10). So it has been God's plan from the beginning to bring about this very thing. History states it, prophecy stipulates it, and Deity seals it as being a divinely determined design.

The reign of this King will be characterized by repleteness of rectitude and by the resplendence of righteousness. All that is vigorous in virility and virtuous in victory has already been personified in the character and conduct of God's King. As a Sovereign, He saves and secures forevermore. As a King, He is also a Kinsman and kindly disposed toward His people. As a

Lord, He loves and leads by living fountains of water. As a Ruler, He reigns and reveals new marvels of mercy continually. As a Prince, He presides in His power and purposes of grace eternally. As a Monarch, He maintains forever and ministers to the myriads that comprise His kingdom. The administrations of His present campaigns are directed to world conquest, which precedes His world control as visualized in Revelation 11:15. We need to feel the force and fervor of His claim the more, grasp the grandeur and glory of His revealed aim, and labor diligently and devotedly in furthering the interests of His kingdom, until the Day dawns and the Daystar arises.

> Come then, and added to Thy many crowns,
>   Receive yet one, the crown of all the earth.
> For thou alone are worthy.
>   It was Thine by ancient covenant, ere nature's birth,
> And Thou hast made it Thine by purchase since,
>   And overpaid its value by Thy blood.
> Come, then, and added to Thy many crowns,
>   Receive this one the crown of matchless worth.
>
>   COWPER

THE KING OF THE JEWS

Where is He that is born King of the Jews? for we have seen His star in the east, and are come to worship Him (Matt. 2:2).

The law of kingship under the Old Testament Covenant is very explicit. According to the divine law no stranger or foreigner was to be selected as king, but a brother of like nationality. Likewise no sport enthusiast, no self-indulgent individual, and no seeker of riches was to be permitted to reign. The king was required to be familiar with the Scriptures and a seeker and follower of the truth (Deut. 17:15-20). No violation of the law was more glaring than when the leaders of Jewry shouted, "We have no king but Caesar." Jerome's reference to this in relating it to Zechariah 11:6 is very striking indeed, and should be carefully weighed in the light of Matthew 21:19. Jesus the just had every qualification and credential for kingship, according to the law of Moses, in which the Jewish people boasted; and yet the leaders of the nation used the very law that commended Him to condemn Him.

The word *Jew* is derived from Judah, of which tribe Christ came according to the flesh (Gen. 49:10; Heb. 7:14). *Judah* means "to appraise, to value or estimate the worthship of anything." Judah expressed himself first in this capacity in Genesis 37:26. David of the tribe of Judah was the greatest appraiser in Israel. His supreme valuation was the estimate he left on record of God's worthiness to receive worship, praise, and adoration, which he himself rendered right worthily. Christ, who came of the seed of David, of the house of David, of the city of David, and as Son of David, and who came to be head of the kingdom of David is the final King of Israel and the last King of the Jews. Wherefore He is the greatest Appraiser, Valuer, and Estimator the world has ever known. He declared the hour was coming when all that were in the graves would hear His voice and come forth and stand at His tribunal, on which occasion their works, good or evil, would receive final appraisement (John 5:29; Rom. 2:16).

No one born into this world previously or since had a more notable witness than Christ did to denote His royal character and regal claims. No Pharaoh of Egypt, no king of Babylon, no emperor of Persia, no philosopher of Greece, no Caesar of Rome, no sultan of Turkey, no caliph of Arabia, no czar of Russia, no kaiser of Germany, no Napoleon of France ever had a new lamp hung in the sky to mark his birth. Christ had the scroll of prophecy to assure, the song of the angels to announce, the scintillating star to attract, the sages from afar to affirm, and numerous other sensational happenings to commemorate the notable event of His never-to-be-forgotten entry into this world.

Strange indeed that when such signal happenings were taking place in fulfillment of age-old predictions, the Jewish leaders did not even bother to go to Bethlehem to see if the report of the Wise Men were true. The supernatural nature of these confirmations is most striking. The prophecies of Scripture were so plain and plentiful, the angel announcement was so clear and comprehensive, the star of direction was so bright and brilliant, the sages from the East were so real and reverent. Every feature contributed and conformed to the law and to the testimony. No part in the occurrences was played in obscurity. Nor was the One born about to commence a career. His ways had been from of old, from everlasting (Mic. 5:2). His kingship manifested here was but a tiny microcosm of the magnificent majesty of the heavenly commonwealth from whence He came. Angelic loyalty had for ages attended His royalty in the kingdom of Heaven. They had sung salutations to this sovereign Lord at the dawn of creation, when He cast forth comets and planets in their spacious orbits, and directed the winds in their circuits.

This special mission of the angels should be carefully pondered. The very tone of their song signified their testimony was true (Ps. 87:5-7). The manner of their appearance definitely assured their announcement to be absolutely accurate. The nature of their praise in itself suggests perfect sincerity. Their very countenances contributed the final confirmation that their communication was correct. Three outstanding occasions are recorded in which the glory of the Lord was displayed. These constituted the period of creation, the place of revelation, and the presence in manifestation. In the creation God is highly dignified in the majesty of His power, in revelation He is more highly magnified in the ministry of His purpose, while in the manifestation He is most highly glorified in the mystery of His passion. This last is the glory that excelleth, for the marvelous visit of Heaven's perfect love which came with the birth of the King of the Jews is God's supremest glory even as announced by the angelic host, "Glory to God in the Highest." This topmost note of praise has continued to echo down through the aisles of the ages.

The Jews have ever been and are men wondered at (Zech. 3:8), and constitute the only community in the world with a continuous life history lasting over four thousand years. Far back beyond the days of Aryan prestige, when imperious Persia marched to conquest, before Greece brought forth her brilliant philosophers, or conceived her renowned culture and art, and before Rome even toddled in rural infancy—before all this Mount Moriah had witnessed the dignified faith of Abraham; Sinai had reverberated with the decalogue of Moses; the Judean hills had reechoed the delightful cadences of Hebrew poetry, and Mount Zion had chanted the majestic music of David's Psalms. From these people, through the revelation of Truth, came the pioneers who opened the highway of access to the Most High, and furnished the fashions of approach to the portals of the celestial and eternal. Revelation was the secret of their national existence and they held in their possession mysterious promises mightier than the combined powers of the entire world could either fulfill or frustrate. In due time the Revealer Himself appeared, the Ruler of precreation days, the Redeemer in person, the Ratifier of the covenant, the Ransomer from the grave, the veritable and venerable King of the Jews, whose ways were from old, from everlasting (Mic. 5:2). Under this title He was shamefully mistried, by the greatest miscarriage of justice ever perpetrated (Mark 15:9-12). Under this title He was mocked, by the meanest methods and most contemptible mimicry (Mark 15:17-20). Under this title He was murdered, crucified between two malefactors of infamy (Mark 15:25-30). We await His return in prevailing majesty (Mark 14:62).

THE KING OF ISRAEL

> Jesus saw Nathanael coming to Him, and saith of him, Behold an Israelite indeed, in whom is no guile! Nathanael saith unto Him, Whence knowest Thou me? Jesus answered and said unto him, Before that Philip called thee, when thou wast under the fig tree, I saw thee. Nathanael answered and saith unto Him, Rabbi, Thou art the Son of God; Thou art the King of Israel (John 1:47-49).

The nation of Israel, of which Christ is the final King, had four specific characteristics which colored the national history and covered the racial economy. We may cite these as comprising a communal society with its code of laws, a celebrated priesthood with its canon of liturgies, a commissioned witness with its charge of liabilities, and a conferred inheritance with its criterion of liberties.

The laws governing the society were the most famous ever legislated for the welfare of a people. On the side of public well-being, there were laws regarding sustentation, recreation, occupation, remuneration, sanitation, segregation, and sterilization. The moral code on the spiritual side surpassed anything known, assuring enlightenment, enablement, endowment, enrichment, enduement, enlargement, and enjoyment on a high level under the jurisdiction of the seven spirits of God.

The celebrated priesthood with its cannon of liturgies enjoined seven national festivals. At the commemoration of each one the high priest varied his robes with a change of official garments, and on each separate occasion one of the seven significant articles of the court and sanctuary were called into the function of the service.

Such an array of types and symbols could not have been established by anyone not possessing the foresight of understanding to know what the types were to typify, and what the symbols were to signify, especially so in that the fulfillment was not to come until centuries later.

The commissioned witness with its liabilities was beautifully illustrated in a seven-knopped lampstand of pure gold. This nation was entrusted with a testimony to seven world empires, in order to make known the character of a coming Messiah who would be King of Israel and Saviour of the world. This function Israel discharged by witnessing to the Egyptian, Syrian, Assyrian, Babylonian, Medo-Persian, Grecian, and Roman empires, each one of which received a clear knowledge of the divinely revealed message.

The conferred inheritance with its criterion of liberties consisted of the land of Palestine, which was divided by lot among the twelve tribes. Its capital city had twelve gates of administration, designed after the pattern of things in the heavens. The greater portion of the Old Testament record is occupied with the operation of this fourfold system of administration. For the purpose of verifying the entire order as being a God-revealed organization, the Son of God and King of Israel appeared in human form. He showed by His ministry and miracles that He was in full exercise of kingly power and authority, and expressed every credential of claim as a regent, together with every qualification of ability as a ruler.

There was not a single virtuous feature of national administration in which He did not function perfectly; and when they accused Him of breaking the Sabbath He replied that He was Lord of the Sabbath, for He inaugurated it. If they questioned Him in regard to temple service He declared, "There is one in this place greater than the temple." When the leaders challenged the wisdom of His words He answered, "Behold, a greater than Solomon is here." The most tragic instance of failure to recognize Him is right here: He came to His own and His own received Him not.

He was thoroughly conversant with every detail relative to the sanctity of the priests, the dignity of the prophets, and the majesty of the kings of Israel. In His ministry He was never cramped or confined by circumstances, nor dependent on human sources of supply. He never attempted to do things that attracted or appealed to the carnal instincts of the race, nor made one solitary suggestion of a material kingdom in this present world. His whole life was exemplary, His heart full of sympathy, His will ever marked by divine sovereignty, and His manner graced with simplicity and mercy. If Christ is not the King of Israel in full accord with every precept and prediction of the Word of God, there cannot and will not ever be such a King. He is the only One who fully magnified the law, completely glorified the truth, wholly ratified the promises, genuinely beautified grace, and finally dignified justice.

The kingly Christ cannot be measured by the standards of earthly kings, or by human sons, or by racial heads, or by national lords. He holds seven kingships, which are dealt with in this chapter. He has seven sonships that span the coverage from Son of man in humanity, to Son of God in deity. He graces seven headships from being Head of every man, to Head of all principality and power, might, and dominion. He administers seven lordships from Lord of the harvest to Lord of Heaven and earth. Our bounden duty is to submit willingly and wholeheartedly to the mastery of His kingship without question or qualification. He is the finality of authority for human dignity, national liberty, and kingly majesty. He has every right to the throne, every title to the inheritance, every claim to the kingdom, and every quality of lordship for eternal dominion.

> King of my life I crown Thee now,
>   Thine shall the glory be;
> Lest I forget Thy thorn-crowned brow,
>   Lead me to Calvary.

J. E. HUSSEY

THE KING OF SAINTS

> Great and marvellous are Thy works, Lord God Almighty; just and true are Thy ways, Thou King of saints. Who shall not fear Thee, O Lord, and glorify Thy name? for Thou only art holy: for all nations shall come and worship before Thee; for Thy judgments are made manifest (Rev. 15:3-4).

As is well known, one manuscript uses king of nations in this portion, and a number of authorities deem it to be correct, because of the character of the message contained in the chapter. However, our Lord said to His own on one occasion, "Fear not, little flock; for it is your Father's good pleasure to give you the kingdom" (Luke 12:32). The saints at Colosse were reminded that they had been translated into the kingdom of God's Son, and where there is a kingdom there must be a king. Daniel likewise affirms, "The saints of the most High shall take the kingdom, and possess the kingdom for ever" (Dan. 7:18). He also assures us that "the Ancient of days came, and judgment was given to the saints of the most High; and the time came that the saints possessed the kingdom" (Dan. 7:22). In the light of these and other references the expression *King of saints* is not irrelevant to this scene of judgment.

Our focus is on the King Himself, for what must His character be like to be King of all the spiritually minded, pure-hearted, wholly consecrated, saintly souls of all the centuries? The divine intent has been clearly expressed that the saints are to be conformed to the image of the Son, and the Son's kingdom is where the saints realize their function (Col. 1:12). Wherefore, Peter teaches us to strive to have an abundant entrance (2 Pet. 1:11).

What are we to comprehend in One so comely of countenance, so holy of heart, so goodly in grace, so sweetly pure, and so kindly of spirit as to be called King of Saints? He Himself is the Regenerator of every saint in the kingdom; He it is who makes each one a partaker of the divine nature. The unlighted luster of His own unlimited glory is entire and eternal; the saints reflect but some of the rays. The underived immortality of His incorruptibility is complete and continual; the saints derive life and immortality from Him. The unimputed righteousness of His perfection is pure and perpetual; the saints receive imputed righteousness and are purified through His redeeming grace. The unbestowed beauty of His holiness is unblemished and abiding, whereas the saints are those He begets again in His divine likeness. The unlit brightness of His brilliant light shines effulgently and everlastingly, but the saints are lit in order to shine as lights in the world. Without controversy Christ is most certainly King of saints.

Saint means a holy one, and He has said, "Be ye holy, for I am holy." In other words, Be ye saintly, for I am saintly. For it doth not yet appear what we shall be, but we know that, when He shall appear, we shall be like Him. Every saint is yet to become a facsimile of Christ, bearing the very virtues of His character, and wearing the impress of His image. The fact of the nature of the life of the chrysalis enwrapped in a drab, unattractive cocoon is the earnest of the transfiguration that will one day transpire. When the day of release dawns, the beauty of the butterfly breaks forth from the rough enclosure.

Christ the King of saints has given to us numerous glimpses in the Scriptures of what is to come and has flashed on the scroll of the covenant gleams of the glory that awaits beyond the material boundaries. What glowing traceries we find of a golden dawn, a cloudless morn, a fadeless day, a tearless state, a thornless paradise, a painless life in a deathless home where we shall see His face and be like Him in His endless kingdom. Sunlight travels over ninety million miles to open the crimson-tipped petals of a common daisy. Profounder far was the distance of a sin-stained soul from a holy God. But the scarlet-tinged sacrificial love of the Most High descended to redeem and deliver, and raise up to seat us with the King of saints in heavenly places. If we really expect one day to resemble our Redeemer we shall exert our utmost effort to reach some partial, practical likeness here and now.

THE KING OF THE AGES

> Now unto the king eternal [of the ages], immortal [incorruptible], invisible, the only wise God, be honour and glory for ever [unto the ages of the ages] and ever (1 Tim. 1:17 Newberry margin).

The light that emanates from the face of Jesus Christ continues to increase with greater beauty and brilliancy. Mighty affirmations are made by this messenger who had himself a marvelous experience of mediatorial mercy when the risen Lord manifested Himself to him on the Damascus road. From the multiform wealth of Christ's attributes, Paul makes a selection which is admirably suited to the subject he is recording. He has just recounted the revealing facts in relation to his remarkable conversion, and the revolutionary change that had taken place in his own life. He relates that by his resolute resistance to everything pertaining to one called Jesus, whose name he sought to erase from the country and expel or execute all those who were adherents of His, he had tried God's patience more than any other individual, and was therefore the chief of sinners. He states that his salvation was a pattern, for if the one who provoked all God's long-suffering was saved, there was hope for all those who had provoked to a lesser degree.

Then, as if startled by the things just described, he breaks forth in an outburst of adoring gratitude, in which he ascribes the honor and glory of these unmerited blessings to the King of the Ages, a title eminently suited to the case in point. He recognizes that the One who flashed upon him those blinding rays of light, more brilliant than the sunshine, was none other than the King of the centuries. What a high and honorable dignity to have a potentate of such caliber interest Himself in a rebellious Pharisee!

Arrayed administratively in almighty authority, there reigns a King who shapes all history, supervises national and personal activities, and molds the very incidents that lead to the arrest and conversion of a sinner. The Authorized rendering, "King eternal," has reference to duration, whereas what the apostle is stressing has reference to One who is directing, designing, and determining the course of events. This King is the framer of the laws of the universe, the One who fashions the ages, who forms the stage and sphere for the enactments of life, and furnishes the very lives of those who play a part in the mysterious drama. The King of the historic ages is likewise King of providence, whose prescient eye enables Him to plan well ahead of time and to provide adequately for the emergency that will arise. There is a Deliverer who acts intelligently, wisely, and correctly because of a full knowledge of all the facts of the case. This is at once revealing, arresting, and consoling.

Do we realize there is a King at the center of this great universe, who in His mystic being and majestic bearing knows and loves and cares, and who is constantly ministering munificent blessings for our present well-being and future welfare? Things which at times appear trivial are yet in the line of a train of events, administered by a Controller who has all power in Heaven and on earth, directing everything toward the achievement of an eternal purpose. This keen-minded magnificent soul, Saul of Tarsus, realized that he was included in the thought and plan of this overseeing, overruling omnipotent King and that his life was being carefully planned. One of the great proofs of the governance of this King down through the ages is verified in the expressions of faith He has prompted and promoted in the lives of His people.

He is the Author of the verity of faith in Adam, the virtue of faith in Eve, the vision of faith in Enoch, the vitality of faith in Noah, the vocation of faith in Seth, the venture of faith in

Abraham, and so on down through the centuries. Christ produces and perfects the faith in each one of these diverse lives. If we require another aspect of His administrative work we may take into account the ability of Moses, the sanctity of Aaron, the activity of Joshua, the ministry of Samuel, the authority of David, the majesty of Solomon, the chivalry of Elijah, the integrity of Ezra, the liberality of Nehemiah, the sympathy of Zechariah, and the fidelity of John the forerunner, together with all the noble characters in between, with a continuity down to the present day. Therefore, notice that the creditable and commendable features of each may be rightly attributed to the King of the historic ages, who declared, "I am Alpha and Omega, the beginning and the ending, saith the Lord, which is, and which was, and which is to come, the Almighty" (Rev. 1:8).

THE KING OF RIGHTEOUSNESS AND PEACE

For this Melchisedec, king of Salem, priest of the most high God, who met Abraham returning from the slaughter of the kings, and blessed him; to whom also Abraham gave a tenth part of all; first being by interpretation King of righteousness, and after that also King of Salem, which is, King of peace . . . made like unto the Son of God (Heb. 7:1-3).

When Christ is considered as a King, the blessedness of His government rises highest, the boundlessness of His grace reaches furthest, and the brightness of his glory shines more brilliant than the sun. He surpasses every other titled celebrity and famed dignitary, and is mightier than all other majesties and princelier than all other potentates. His wisdom is infinite, His dominion absolute, His knowledge perfect, and His power complete.

The mysterious manifestation of this patriarchal king, Melchisedec, to Abraham on the plains of Mamre, furnishes some more interesting material which, in turn, further magnifies the magnificent majesty of Messiah, the Prince of kings. To extol the fame of Christ's kingship, two renowned orders of priesthood are chosen and contrasted. In the Aaronic order a pedigree was required and parentage had to be submitted before a priest was consecrated. In the Melchisedec order the King of Salem was without mother, without father, and without descent, having neither beginning of days, nor end of life, but made like to the Son of God.

The Aaronic order had a succession of appointed priests, while in Melchisedec there was neither predecessor nor successor. The Aaronic office was held for a stated period of thirty years, whereas the Melchisedec order was continuous and indestructible. These, together with other notable contrasts, are given. As priest of the Most High this mediator was king of righteousness and peace; that is, he personified both. In the case of Christ's kingliness, righteousness is not a principle or standard, but the personality, the sovereignty, the Lord our righteousness (Jer. 23:6). Furthermore, peace is not a compact, but a character, for of Christ it is written, He is our peace (Eph. 2:14).

The description given directs us to One who is exceptionally imperial, essentially immutable, and eternally invariable. In the text the term *King of Salem* does not refer to a locality but a quality of soul, not to a country but a celebrity.

The two great features of kingship reflected here are perfectly expressed in Christ. He is rightful and faithful in all exercise of authority, because He is righteousness personified. He is peaceful and graceful in every feature of activity, because He is peace personalized. Christ has purposed to establish peace, therefore He believes in it absolutely. Peace at any price, even at the price of war. In righteousness He doth judge and make war (Rev. 19:11). The scene described is the final victory over rebel kings, of which the initial defeat is described in Genesis 14.

The special honor Christ receives is due to His superior nature; the essence of His essential kingship is underived and is never transmitted to another. He exercises powers no one else can wield, He expresses perfections no one else can portray, He exhibits prerogatives no one else can use, and He enjoys privileges to which no one else holds title.

Of Melchisedec it is written, Now consider how great this man was, to whom Abraham paid homage and in return received hospitality and the honor of being blessed by him, without all contradiction the less was blessed of the better. Then in such light, have we considered how great the Man Christ Jesus is, the King of Heaven, the King of glory, the King of kings? Have we considered how great He is in His noteworthy name and nature and nobility? Have we considered how great He is in His power to govern, His prerogative to bless, and His preeminence to rule and reign? Have we considered how great He is in the depths of His love, the degrees of His wisdom, the dimensions of His might, and the designs of His purpose? The blaze of this King's brilliance is blinding, the orbit of His office is overwhelming, and the arch of His authority is astounding.

So wholly superior in personality, He is a King kindly disposed toward His people, a sovereign Saviour, majestic in mercy, superior in sympathy, perfect in pity, and withal most bountiful in blessing. A greater, higher, nobler than Melchisedec is here.

Three specific features are necessary in a durable kingdom, namely, righteousness, peace, and joy. These are three of the unshakable things that remain when all things that can be shaken shall be shaken (Heb. 12:27). Wherefore, Isaiah speaks of everlasting righteousness, ever-abiding peace, and everlasting joy. Christ is appointed King by an almighty oath, and at the same time is anointed with the oil of joy above all. This completes the trio: He is King of righteousness and peace, anointed with the oil of joy. Therefore the requisites of the everlasting kingdom reside in Him bodily. Well did He say during His manifestation, "The kingdom of God is within [in the midst of] you" (Luke 17:21 Newberry margin). He is the Righteousness, He is the Peace, He is the Joy, the entire kingdom in expression. This is the King who is in a position and condition to show everlasting kindness (Isa. 54:8).

THE KING OF HEAVEN

> I, Nebuchadnezzar, praise and extol and honour the King of heaven, all whose works are truth, and His ways judgment: and those that walk in pride He is able to abase.
>
> I praised and honoured Him that liveth for ever, whose dominion is an everlasting dominion (Dan. 4:37,34).

Revelation from Heaven is not the result of human resolution. In His stately sovereignty the King of Heaven holds the prerogative to reveal unseen realities. The highest knowledge is to know the Father; Christ alone can reveal such knowledge (Matt. 11:27).

This King does "according to His will in the army of heaven and among the inhabitants of the earth, and none can stay His hand or say unto Him, What doest Thou?" (Dan. 4:35) The character of this King stands in sharp contrast to that of the kings of the earth. This holds true in a wide variety of notable characteristics. The immutability of His wisdom, His will, and His word outclasses and outvies all earthly authorities. The immensity of His dignity and range of dominion dim into insignificance the dominions of this world. The immunity experienced from disaster, defeat, and destruction throughout the entire domain distinguishes His kingdom from all others. The immeasurability of the King's might and majesty never diminishes or decays; He reigns forever and ever (Dan. 7:18). The immortality that characterizes the perfection of the administration assures the permanence of the power and the perennial pleasure that prevails, free from all disaffection and disruption. The infinity of the King's personal glory and beauty outshines in luster and luminosity all lesser lights in the expansive hierarchy and extensive honor of the Heaven of heavens.

The eternal features are of such magnitude, no being in existence can derange one single cog in the wheels of His potential prerogatives and prevailing providences. The reign of His omnipotence extends everywhere over everyone everlastingly. His title of kingship can never vanish away, His throne of majesty will never be vacant, His truth remains, and can never be vanquished. The King of Heaven is without variableness and His throne is free of all vulnerability. As King He ever lives, ever loves, and ever lasts. He held this high and honorable office ages before His manifestation, as He said when tried, "Mv kingdom is not of this world."

Earth's kings depend on innumerable external agencies for strength and security and even then they last but a short time. The King of Heaven is from everlasting to everlasting. Stars and seas, mountains and meadows, times and seasons do not contribute one whit to the maintenance or magnificence of the sovereignty and superiority of Heaven's King. He is eternal though all else be temporal, He is impregnable though all else be vulnerable, He is immortal though all else be corruptible. Of Him it is written, "Thou remainest." We may resort to the remotest records without avail, for human standards of measurement cannot estimate His everabiding majesty.

In the Old Testament Scriptures, upwards of six hundred twenty references appear concerning Heaven and the heavens. Seven of these are expressed in the superlative degree, the first by Moses in the Pentateuch: "Behold, the heaven and the heaven of heavens is the Lord's thy God, the earth also, with all that therein is" (Deut. 10:14). Solomon made reference to this in His dedicatory prayer for the temple: "Behold, the heaven and heaven of heavens cannot contain Thee; how much less this house that I have builded?" (1 Kings 8:27) David in the psalm in which he describes the ascension of Christ. whom he addresses as "My God, my king" (Psalm 68:24), increases the intensiveness by saying, "Sing unto God. ve kingdoms of the earth; O sing praises unto the Lord; Selah: to Him that rideth upon the heavens of heavens" (68:32-33). Nehemiah adds yet another note: "Thou, even Thou, art Lord alone; Thou hast made heaven, the heaven of heavens, with all their host . . . and the host of heaven worshipeth Thee" (Neh. 9:6).

In these undefinable realms the Lord has prepared and established His throne. The immensity of His magnificence and the immortality of His majesty are wholly inexpressible. When Paul was caught up into the third heaven and had a glimpse of the celestial court, he said he saw things that could not be lawfully uttered, meaning by this that all our known laws of magnitude and standards for measuring magnificence are outlawed and violated, because of the inconceivable glory. Such terms as profoundness of perfection, exceptional excellencies, and marvelous magnificence are poverty-stricken words in relation to such transcendent glory. We are told that the host of Heaven is innumerable, then how could the human mind estimate maintenance costs? Such terms as splendors and gorgeous grandeurs are too weak to describe the indescribable.

We should ever remember that in Christ there is a degree of excellence held in reserve which is exclusively for the pleasure of God the Father. This portion of His infinite perfection is beyond the capacity of the redeemed of the Lord to perceive or appropriate, and is a subject for adoring worship.

As King of Heaven, Christ has many diadems (Rev. 19:12), and He is fairest in beauty, noblest in dignity, loveliest in majesty, and holiest in mercy. As King of Heaven, He wears the most distinguished diadem of deathless dominion. His imperishable merit and impenetrable worthiness mount highest in ceaseless fame. On His brow rests the choicest coronet of charming comeliness, while His hand sways the sublimest scepter of supreme strength ever wielded in righteousness. His unfailing faithfulness and unvarying constancy qualify Him to reign forever and ever in an undefiled, unfading dominion that has a length, breadth, depth, and height that surpasseth knowledge.

> Praise, my soul, the King of Heaven,
>   To His feet thy tribute bring,
> Ransomed, healed, restored, forgiven,
>   Who like thee His praise should sing.
>
> Sinners in derision crowned Him,
>   Mocking thus the Saviour's claim.
> Saints and angels crowd around Him,
>   Own His title, praise His name.

For the high mysteries of Thy name
The creature's grasp transcend,
The Father only (glorious claim!)
The Son can comprehend.

                J. CONDOR

THE KING OF GLORY

Lift up your heads, O ye gates; and be ye lift up, ye
everlasting doors; and the King of glory shall come in. Who is
this King of glory? The Lord strong and mighty, the Lord
mighty in battle (Ps. 24:7-8).

Blessed be God for permitting us a transient glance at the
circumstances attending the stateliest of triumphant entries,
the entry of the kingliest sovereign Victor into the eternal city.
The ascension glory as portrayed in Psalm 68 is overwhelming.
This brief but brilliant description, given in a few masterful
strokes, helps us to visualize in part the portly proceedings of
that august occasion.

"Thy glory is above the heavens" is thrice repeated in the
Psalms. Here the King of Glory ascends the throne of the
heavens at the utmost pinnacle of power, in preeminent
perfection of state, transportingly transcendent. Glory is the
crowning diadem of all the attributes of deity. The Scriptures
teach that holiness, righteousness, faithfulness, goodness,
graciousness, loving-kindness, and all such virtues are glory-
crowned. Presiding in kingly dignity over the total aggregate
of the entire range is the King of Glory.

Anticipating the glorious climax expressed in the psalm
from which we derive our heading, let us notice the sequence
of thought which leads to the tremendous issue. Psalm 22 pictures the sacrificial Substitute for salvation, and His Name
and His righteousness are declared (verses 22,31). Psalm 23
portrays the spiritual Shepherd for sustentation, who leads in
the paths of righteousness for His Name's sake, thus combin-
ing the twofold declaration of Psalm 22. Psalm 24 presents the
sacerdotal sovereign for sanctification, and the righteousness

and name, *King of Glory,* complete the portraiture. The Substitute becomes the Shepherd in resurrection sufficiency, and the Shepherd ascends to the throne of sovereignty and assures satisfaction forevermore.

The far-flung range covered in Psalm 24 is worthy of special interest. The opening portion deals with the habitable world and its fullness. (*Habitable* is the Hebrew word that is used.) Here we meet the first exhibition of glory in creation. Paul the apostle affirms that "the glory of the celestial is one, and the glory of the terrestrial is another." There is one glory of the sun and another glory of the moon, and another glory of the stars (1 Cor. 15:40-41).

Following this material glory the psalm advances to the sphere of moral glory, and names the hill of the Lord and the holy place and also states the qualifications for entrance—a heart of purity and hands free from defilement. Both these aspects are then superseded by celestial glory, when the heads of the hoary gates of heavenly portals heave in sight and the spiritual hosts within come into view. The escort associated with the triumphal entry is mentioned in Psalm 68:17. What an entourage! At the center of the circle of celebrities, coronated in captivating beauty and enthroned in consummate majesty sits the King of Glory. His glory extends, expands, encompasses, and exceeds in every way thinkable. In this select and stately office Christ stands exclusively alone. Nowhere in the whole realm of knowledge do we find a claimant who assumes the highest station, King of Glory. This One is mightiest in authority, chiefest in chivalry, strongest in virility, and worthiest in victory.

Does it seem incredible to you that the King of Glory had the right to request the Father to send Him more than twelve legions of angels? (Matt. 26:53-54) We should reverently admire the glorious reticence and self-restraint of Him who held the prerogative to call embattled hosts, as a personal bodyguard, in all their glittering strength and girded might, with ranks of helmed cherubim and sworded seraphim, to His aid for self-defense, but declined to do so. What self-restraint is this! Yet by His submission to the Father's will He subdued and conquered the strongest foe. The Anointed of the Most High was accustomed to massive honors before He appeared in human form, and yet He submitted to being maligned and maltreated by the menial of earth. Amazing patience, astounding grace, and love beyond compare.

> When I survey the wondrous Cross
>   On which the King of Glory died,
> My richest gain I count but loss,
>   And pour contempt on all my pride.
>
> Were the whole realm of nature mine,
>   That were an offering far too small;
> Love so amazing, so divine,
>   Demands my heart, my life, my all!
>   ISAAC WATTS

Never before in any title possessed by any potentate do we find the combination in which such intensity of radiance is linked with such immensity of range. Never at any period of history do we find greater integrity of heart joined to such infinity of honor as witnessed here. Never in the records of the years was there anyone in closer intimacy of kinship with mankind, who ascended to such heights of immortality in kingship, to reign over all. The very weight of His impartial merit qualifies Him to lay hold of incorruptible might as King of Glory.

How wonderful it is to contemplate that the prevalence of His personal love for the sons of men, and the relevance of His preeminent lordship in heavenly majesty are now united forever, under one almighty scepter.

Both James and John, in their writings, speak of Christ as the glory, while Paul refers to Him as the Lord of glory, indicating that He not only reigns in authority as King, but that He administers also as Lord. In relation to both of these supreme offices, the superlatives are used in the New Testament, where He is declared King of kings and Lord of lords, and this pertains to the highest and holiest sphere, the Heaven of heavens.

Therefore Christ holds a higher regency than was ever known by the sovereigns of earth. He has nobler majesty than that which marks the royalties of men. He heads a vaster dynasty than could be amassed by all the kingdoms of the world in one. He is anointed with the oil of joy above His companions, so that in vitality, energy, and ecstasy He transcends.

THE KING OF KINGS

On His head were many crowns [diadems]. . . . And He hath on His vesture and on His thigh a name written, King of kings, and Lord of lords (Rev. 19:12,16).

When David conquered Rabbah of Ammon, he took the king's crown which was made of gold and precious stones, and placed it upon his own head (2 Sam. 12:30). Ptolemy entered Antioch wearing the crown of Asia and Egypt. In 1385, the Prince of Wales adopted the crown of King John of the Bohemians after the victory gained at the battle of Cressy. Inscribed beneath three ornamental feathers were the words, *Ich Dien*, I serve, which were adopted by the royal house of Great Britain as a motto for the crown prince. But here we view a greater battlefield and a grander victory, and the Conqueror is adorned with the many diadems of His multiform victories, of vaster value than any ever gained by man.

As we proceed with our investigation we discover richer, fuller, higher qualities packed into the many variegated titles of our blessed Lord and beloved Saviour. None but Christ could ever lay claim to seven kingships, but He is King of the Jews, King of Israel, King of righteousness, King of the ages, King of saints, King of Heaven, King of glory, and over and above all, King of kings. Such range of regality was never before appended to the head of any monarch, for every realm of importance is included—racial, national, spiritual, ecclesiastical, historical, celestial, and supernal. His authority is the more massive in magnitude because of the unvarying sufficiency and unwavering stability of His trustworthy throne. Goodness, faithfulness, righteousness, and holiness form the main foundations of His administration.

The Administrator Himself in His kingly stature, lovely nature, and friendly gesture surpasses all others in His perfect ability and absolute control. His trackless riches, endless resources, and exhaustless reserves assure His age-abiding authority. The prodigious measure of His manifold treasure does not consist merely of precious metals but of peerless merit. His amalgamated treasure is not in gold but grace, not in money but mercy, not in lore but love, not in trade but truth, not in values but virtues, not in silver wealth but sterling worth. The human mind cannot conceive the delectability of His changeless character, which is without variableness; nor comprehend the desirability of His stainless life, which is without blemish; nor calculate the durability of His matchless love, which is without partiality. When He officially takes hold of the reins of national government (Ps. 22:28), there will be no lessening of the light of truth, no languishing in the life of faith, and no limiting the forward march of love's eternal triumph. With new perceptive eyes we shall continually behold the fresh unfoldings of His radiant glory, in all its amaranthine beauty and brightness.

Who is there on earth capable of compiling an inventory of the invested interests of the King of kings which He has placed in hundreds of millions of redeemed lives with their concrete affection and complete devotion? How can we estimate the King's income from regenerated hearts in their offering of perfect praise untainted with hypocrisy, their worthy worship unblemished by wrangling, holy homage unmarred by feigning, and ardent adoration unsullied by insincerity or double-mindedness.

Where may we obtain a surveyor to calculate or tabulate the areas of the vast estate of the King's eternal inheritance, to say nothing of His lasting legacy of the Father's love, the longevity of His everlasting dominion, or even the liabilities of maintenance in upholding all things by the word of His power?

Upon this King of kings devolves the stupendous task of administering the power which governs innumerable starry constellations, the prodigious hierarchies of angels, and the fabulous millions of perfected saints, every feature of whose immortal lives He caters for and controls in absolute harmony, amity, and unity. The retinue of His celestial court is awe- inspiring, the revenue of the better country is incalculable, while the residue of His tribute from the holy city baffles all our standards of descriptive utterance.

If ever an occasion arises in the hereafter in which the redeemed hosts will need to be strengthened with might by His Spirit in the inner man, to comprehend the dimensions of divine glory, it will be when the investiture of the King of kings is unveiled before the greatest assemblage of admirers ever gathered. These hosts shall be summoned from the remotest bound of the entire universe to God, by means of that instant transit known to the omnipotent One. The millionfold praise from myriads of myriads shall be presented to the Premier of personalities, the sole President of principalities, and the one Prince of potentates.

> King of kings and Lord of lords,
> Oh, how rich these glorious words,
> Titles high, with boundless fame,
> Now enhance the Saviour's name.
>
> J. WILSON SMITH

If we search the galleries of the great, seeking the most famous of historic and heroic veterans, we should certainly remember this worthiest of warriors who towers loftily above all others. The fact that Christ is already coronated at the right hand of the Majesty in the heavens the chiefest of chieftains, carries the assurance that at the time of His exaltation, every attribute of deity, every excellence of perfection, and every gracious virtue was crowned with Him. His preeminent province as the Regent of royalties, the Magister of masters, the Monarch of magnates, the Commandant of commanders, the Leader of leaderships, the Governor of governorships, the Lord of lordships, and the King of kingships reminds us that He is higher than the Heaven of heavens, holier than the holy of holies, and adorned with a heavier weight of honor than all the honorable of earth combined.

Christ testified of John the herald, that he was the greatest born of women; yet John frankly admitted that he was not worthy to loosen His Lord's shoelace, and he thrice emphasized that Christ had precedence over Him. Then, may we ask, what kind of a King must Christ be whose remoteness in royal power and whose abysmal depths of regal might preceded creation? Wherefore, Moses in his day was not exceeding the bounds of rhetoric when he described the unrivaled splendor of Messiah by asking, "Who is like Thee, glorious in holiness, fearful in praises, doing wonders?" (Ex. 15:11)

This King magnifies the greatest magnitude, multiplies the extremest measures, and glorifies the zenith of glory, as the Sovereign of all statesmen.

His infinite being is the home of the highest and holiest in the excellencies of meekness, the sweetest and strongest in the virtues of righteousness, the lowliest and loveliest in the beauties of holiness. Therefore we may say most certainly that He is King of kings in whose splendors of personality the glories of the supernatural are enshrined in their fadeless beauty.

> Look ye saints! The sight is glorious:
> See the Man of sorrows now,
> From the fight returned victorious:
> Every knee to Him shall bow.
> Crown Him! Crown Him! Crown Him! Crown Him!
> Crowns become the Victor's brow.

* * *

> Hark! those bursts of acclamation!
> Hark! those loud triumphant chords!
> Jesus takes the highest station;
> O what joy the sight affords.
> Crown Him! Crown Him! Crown Him! Crown Him!
> King of kings and Lord of lords.

THOMAS KELLY

Let it be borne in mind that during His ministry as Son of man, the Lord adopted and appropriated, as pertaining to Himself, the names and titles predicted in the Old Testament

Scriptures concerning a Messiah that was to come. Daniel the prophet, while praying for his people and the city of Jerusalem, received a visit from Michael the archangel, who informed him of the time of the Messiah's manifestation to Israel (Dan. 9:25). John the herald bore witness that this took place. "I knew Him not: but that He should be made manifest to Israel, therefore am I come. . . . Upon whom thou shalt see the Spirit descending, and remaining on Him, the same is He" (John 1:31-34). Later, when cast into prison, John sent a deputation to Christ to ask, "Art Thou He that should come, or do we look for another?" (Matt. 11:3)

John the herald had witnessed faithfully of Christ for about six months, but Christ did not visit him when he was imprisoned, nor make any attempt or pray for his release. This doubtless had been the cause of John's inquiry, for he may at least have expected a word of assurance or appreciation.

Christ had declared Himself to be, and was declared to be Messiah, "we have found Him, of whom Moses in the law, and the prophets, did write" (John 1:45). "I know that Messias cometh, which is called Christ: when He is come, He will tell us all things. Jesus saith to her, I that speak unto thee am He" (John 4:25-26). Christ also affirmed that He was the Son of God (John 8:35-36; 9:35-37; 10:35-36); and made many other claims, all of which were verified by the Father, the Holy Spirit, the apostles, and by wonderful signs.

Our Lord knew the real value and vast range of meaning involved in His statements of claim. His very manner indicated that He was conscious He had a perfect right to make claims no one else had ever made, or could make. He declared, "I am the truth"; and besides set Himself forth as the source and center of light, life, love, power, wisdom, grace, and every other attribute. When doing so He consistently linked these with that which is everlasting. The same is true of the many vocations He fulfilled during His manifestation of Saviourhood, Servanthood, Priesthood, Shepherdhood, and suchlike, all of which were foreseen and foretold by the prophets. Furthermore, Christ left no room for a second fulfillment of these prophecies, as advocated by the Jesuit writer Cornelius a Lapidae in his book, *The Law of Double Fulfillment in Prophecy*. Christ did not apply the predictions of the prophets to Himself, as though He but partially and tentatively fulfilled them; but did so as being their final objective, completely and eternally. The Apostle John had revealed to him, when on the Isle of Patmos, the real substance of all shadows, sacrifices, and symbols, as to their original beauty, in the glorious person of the Son of man. From Scriptures which describe His superior excellence of character we shall make a few observations.

We cannot *exalt* Him, for He ascended up far above all heavens; and has a Name above every name (Eph. 4:10; Phil. 2:9).

We cannot *adorn* Him, for He is altogether lovely, the chiefest among ten thousand (5:10,16).

We cannot *enrich* Him, for in Him are hid all the treasures of wisdom and knowledge; He has riches in glory (Col. 2:9; Phil. 4:19).

We cannot *engrace* Him, for He is full of grace and truth; of His fullness have all we received and grace for grace (John 1:14,16).

We cannot *instruct* Him, for He is omniscient and knoweth all things (John 16:30), with whom took He counsel, and instructed Him (Isa. 40:14; Ro. 11:3-4).

We cannot *improve* Him, for He is perfect in kingliness and kindliness, in loftiness and loveliness, in greatness and goodness, in holiness and helpfulness.

We cannot *decorate* Him, for He is divinely desirable and also the desire of all nations (Hag 2:7). How great is His beauty (Zech. 11:17), the beauty of holiness.

We cannot *ornament* Him, for He is the originator of all colorful design in all flowers of the field, fruits of the farm, and foliage of the forest; the Author of flaming sunsets and fascinating dawns. Himself, more glorious than His works.

We cannot *enlighten* Him, for He is the true light, which lighteth every man, the light of the world; and the light of life (John 1:9; 8:12). He is the light of the knowledge of the glory of God (2 Cor. 4:6). His understanding is infinite (Ps. 147:5).

We cannot *confine* Him, for the Heaven of heavens cannot contain Him (1 Kgs 8:27). He is before all things, by Him all things consist (Col. 1:17). He upholdeth all things (Heb. 1:3).

We cannot *promote* Him, for He is preeminent in all (Col. 1:18). Far above all principality, and power, and might, and dominion, and every name that is named (Eph. 1:21): King of kings, Lord of lords (1 Tim. 6:16), Prince of princes (Dan. 8:25).

We cannot *ennoble* Him, for He is enthroned at the summit of sovereignty, and is glorious in majesty, at the very highest state of honor.

We cannot *embellish* Him, for He is excellent as the cedars (S. of Sol. 5:15). His countenance is as effulgent as the Sun (Rev. 1:16). He is the brightness of the Father's glory, radiant in everlasting light (Heb. 1:3; Isa. 60; 10:20).

We cannot *beautify* Him, for He is the Beloved Bridegroom and is like a jasper and sardonyx stone; He is to be seen seated upon a rainbow-circled throne, crowned with diadems (Rev. 4:3; 19:7).

We have sought to trace a little of our Lord's unrivaled majesty, His unbounded authority, His unblemished beauty, and His unsullied glory; but what a small measure of His fullness is really comprehended. He not only satisfies the heart, but ravishes the mind and gratifies the will. In Him, who is the fullness of Godhead bodily, we discover all that is permanent and pleasurable; all that is lovely and likeable; all that is precious and preferable; and all that is divine and desirable. As it is written, "Who of God is made unto us wisdom and righteousness and sanctification and redemption." Wherefore, "He that glorieth, let him glory in the Lord" (1 Cor. 1:30-31).